THE ANNOTATED SHAKESPEARE

Julius Caesar

William Shakespeare

Fully annotated, with an Introduction, by Burton Raffel

With an essay by Harold Bloom

dialogue - a conversation with 2 or more people

monologue - one person talking to others

soliloquy - when one person alone talks to either the
sililoquy audience or themselves

THE ANNOTATED SHAKESPEARE

Yale University Press • *New Haven and London*

Harold Bloom, Introduction to *Julius Caesar*, copyright © 1994, adapted
and reprinted with permission of Chelsea House Publishers, an imprint
of Infobase Publishing.

Designed by Rebecca Gibb.
Set in Bembo type by The Composing Room of Michigan, Inc.
Printed in the United States of America

Library of Congress Cataloging-in-Publication Data
Shakespeare, William, 1564–1616.
Julius Caesar/ William Shakespeare ; fully annotated, with an introduction,
by Burton Raffel ; with an essay by Harold Bloom.
p.   cm.—(The annotated Shakespeare)
Includes bibliographical references (p.   ).
ISBN-13: 978-0-300-10809-5 (pbk.)
ISBN-10: 0-300-10809-5 (pbk.)
1. Caesar, Julius—Assassination—Drama.   2. Conspiracies—Drama.
3. Assassins—Drama.   4. Rome—Drama.   I. Raffel, Burton.
II. Bloom, Harold.   III. Title.
PR2808.A2R26 2006
822.3'3—dc22
2006007378

A catalogue record for this book is available from the British Library.

10 9 8 7 6 5 4 3

For John G. Kulka

CONTENTS

ABOUT THIS BOOK

I n act 2, scene 1, Brutus is observed reading aloud from an anonymous document thrown through his window:

"Brutus, thou sleep'st. Awake, and see thyself.
Shall Rome, etcetera. Speak, strike, redress!
Brutus, thou sleep'st: awake!"
Such instigations have been often dropped
Where I have took them up.
"Shall Rome, etcetera." Thus must I piece it out:
Shall Rome stand under one man's awe? What, Rome?
My ancestors did from the streets of Rome
The Tarquin drive, when he was called a king.
"Speak, strike, redress!" Am I entreated
To speak and strike? O Rome, I make thee promise:
If the redress will follow, thou receivest
Thy full petition at the hand of Brutus!

This was perfectly understandable, we must assume, to the mostly very average persons who paid to watch Elizabethan plays. But who today can make full or comfortable sense of it? In this very fully annotated edition, I therefore present this passage, not in the bare form quoted above, but thoroughly supported by bottom-of-the-page notes:

"Brutus, thou sleep'st. Awake, and see thyself.
Shall Rome, etcetera. Speak, strike, redress![1]
Brutus, thou sleep'st: awake!"
Such instigations[2] have been often dropped
Where I have took[3] them up.
"Shall Rome, etcetera." Thus must I piece it out:[4]
Shall Rome stand[5] under one man's awe? What, Rome?
My ancestors did from the streets of Rome
The Tarquin drive, when he was called a king.[6]
"Speak, strike, redress!" Am I entreated
To speak and strike? O Rome, I make thee promise:[7]
If the redress will follow, thou receivest
Thy full petition[8] at the hand of Brutus!

Without full explanation of words that have over the years shifted in meaning, and usages that have been altered, neither the modern reader nor the modern listener is likely to be equipped for anything like full comprehension.

I believe annotations of this sort create the necessary bridges, from Shakespeare's four-centuries-old English across to ours.

1 restore, reestablish
2 goading, incitements
3 took = taken = picked
4 piece it out = complete/extend it
5 remain, stay
6 see act 1, scene 2, n.108
7 make thee promise = declare to/assure you
8 prayer, request

Some readers, to be sure, will be able to comprehend unusual, historically different meanings without any glosses. Those not familiar with the modern meaning of particular words will easily find clear, simple definitions in any modern dictionary. But most readers are not likely to understand Shakespeare's intended meaning, absent such glosses as I here offer.

There are no serious textual problems, since the only Renaissance text of the play is the 1623 *Folio,* which I have here followed.

My annotation practices have followed the same principles used in *The Annotated Milton,* published in 1999, and in my annotated editions of *Hamlet,* published (as the initial volume in this series) in 2003, *Romeo and Juliet* (published in 2004), and subsequent volumes in this series. Classroom experience has validated these editions. Classes of mixed upper-level undergraduates and graduate students have more quickly and thoroughly transcended language barriers than ever before. This allows the teacher, or a general reader without a teacher, to move more promptly and confidently to the nonlinguistic matters that have made Shakespeare and Milton great and important poets.

It is the inevitable forces of linguistic change, operant in all living tongues, which have inevitably created such wide degrees of obstacles to ready comprehension—not only sharply different meanings, but subtle, partial shifts in meaning that allow us to think we understand when, alas, we do not. Speakers of related languages like Dutch and German also experience this shifting of the linguistic ground. Like early Modern English (ca. 1600) and the Modern English now current, those languages are too close for those who know only one language, and not the other, to be readily able always to recognize what they correctly understand

and what they do not. When, for example, a speaker of Dutch says, "Men kofer is kapot," a speaker of German will know that something belonging to the Dutchman is broken ("kapot" = "kaputt" in German, and "men" = "mein"). But without more linguistic awareness than the average person is apt to have, the German speaker will not identify "kofer" ("trunk" in Dutch) with "Körper"—a modern German word meaning "physique, build, body." The closest word to "kofer" in modern German, indeed, is "Scrankkoffer," which is too large a leap for ready comprehension. Speakers of different Romance languages (French, Spanish, Italian), and all other related but not identical tongues, all experience these difficulties, as well as the difficulty of understanding a text written in their own language five, or six, or seven hundred years earlier. Shakespeare's English is not yet so old that it requires, like many historical texts in French and German, or like Old English texts—for example, *Beowulf*—a modern translation. Much poetry evaporates in translation: language is immensely particular. The sheer *sound* of Dante in thirteenth-century Italian is profoundly worth preserving. So too is the sound of Shakespeare.

I have annotated prosody (metrics) only when it seemed truly necessary or particularly helpful. Readers should have no problem with the silent "e" in past participles (loved, returned, missed). Except in the few instances where modern usage syllabifies the "e," whenever an "e" in Shakespeare is *not* silent, it is marked "è." The notation used for prosody, which is also used in the explanation of Elizabethan pronunciation, follows the extremely simple form of my *From Stress to Stress: An Autobiography of English Prosody* (see "Further Reading," near the end of this book). Syllables with metrical stress are capitalized; all other syllables are in lowercase letters. I have managed to employ normalized Elizabethan spellings, in most indications of pronunciation, but I have sometimes been obliged to deviate, in the higher interest of being understood.

I have annotated, as well, a limited number of such other matters, sometimes of interpretation, sometimes of general or historical relevance, as have seemed to me seriously worthy of inclusion. These annotations have been most carefully restricted: this is not intended to be a book of literary commentary. It is for that reason that the glossing of metaphors has been severely restricted. There is almost literally no end to discussion and/or analysis of metaphor, especially in Shakespeare. To yield to temptation might well be to double or triple the size of this book—and would also change it from a historically oriented language guide to a work of an unsteadily mixed nature. In the process, I believe, neither language nor literature would be well or clearly served.

Where it seemed useful, and not obstructive of important textual matters, I have modernized spelling, including capitalization. Spelling is not on the whole a basic issue, but punctuation and lineation must be given high respect. The Folio uses few exclamation marks or semicolons, which is to be sure a matter of the conventions of a very different era. Still, our modern preferences cannot be lightly substituted for what is, after a fashion, the closest thing to a Shakespeare manuscript we are likely ever to have. We do not know whether these particular seventeenth-century printers, like most of that time, were responsible for question marks, commas, periods, and, especially, all-purpose colons, or whether these particular printers tried to follow their handwritten sources. Nor do we know if those sources, or what part thereof, might have been in Shakespeare's own hand. But in spite of these equivocations and uncertainties, it remains true that, to a very considerable extent, punctuation tends to result from just how the mind responsible for that punctuating *hears* the text. And twenty-first-century minds have no business, in such matters, overruling seventeenth-century ones. Whoever the compositors were, they were more or less Shakespeare's contemporaries, and we are not.

Accordingly, when the original printed text uses a comma, we are being signaled that *they* (whoever "they" were) heard the text, not coming to a syntactic stop, but continuing to some later stopping point. To replace commas with editorial periods is thus risky and on the whole an undesirable practice. (The dramatic action of a tragedy, to be sure, may require us, for twenty-first-century readers, to highlight what four-hundred-year-old punctuation standards may not make clear—and may even, at times, misrepresent.)

When the printed text has a colon, what we are being signaled is that *they* heard a syntactic stop—though not necessarily or even usually the particular kind of syntactic stop we associate, today, with the colon. It is therefore inappropriate to substitute editorial commas for original colons. It is also inappropriate to employ editorial colons when *their* syntactic usage of colons does not match ours. In general, the closest thing to *their* syntactic sense of the colon is our (and their) period.

The printed interrogation (question) marks, too, merit extremely respectful handling. In particular, editorial exclamation marks should very rarely be substituted for interrogation marks.

It follows from these considerations that the movement and sometimes the meaning of what we must take to be Shakespeare's *play* will at times be different, depending on whose punctuation we follow, *theirs* or our own. I have tried, here, to use the printed seventeenth-century text as a guide to both *hearing* and *understanding* what Shakespeare wrote.

Since the original printed texts (there not being, as there never are for Shakespeare, any surviving manuscripts) are frequently careless as well as self-contradictory, I have been relatively free with the wording of stage directions—and in some cases have added brief directions, to indicate who is speaking to whom. I have made no emendations; I have necessarily been obliged to make choices. Textual decisions have been annotated when the differences between or among the original printed texts seem either marked or of unusual interest.

In the interests of compactness and brevity, I have employed in my annotations (as consistently as I am able) a number of stylistic and typographical devices:

- The annotation of a single word does not repeat that word

- The annotation of more than one word repeats the words being annotated, which are followed by an equals sign and then by the annotation; the footnote number in the text is placed after the last of the words being annotated

- In annotations of a single word, alternative meanings are usually separated by commas; if there are distinctly different ranges of meaning, the annotations are separated by arabic numerals inside parentheses—(1), (2), and so on; in more complexly worded annotations, alternative meanings expressed by a single word are linked by a forward slash, or solidus: /

- Explanations of textual meaning are not in parentheses; comments about textual meaning are

- Except for proper nouns, the word at the beginning of all annotations is in lower case

- Uncertainties are followed by a question mark, set in parentheses: (?)

- When particularly relevant, "translations" into twenty-first-century English have been added, in parentheses

- Annotations of repeated words are *not* repeated. Explanations of the *first* instance of such common words are followed by the sign ⋆. Readers may easily track down the first annotation, using the brief Finding List at the back of the book. Words with entirely separate meanings are annotated *only* for meanings no longer current in Modern English.

The most important typographical device here employed is the sign ⋆ placed after the first (and only) annotation of words and phrases occurring more than once. There is an alphabetically arranged listing of such words and phrases in the Finding List at the back of the book. The Finding List contains no annotations but simply gives the words or phrases themselves and the numbers of the relevant act, the scene within that act, and the footnote number within that scene for the word's first occurrence.

The editors of the 1623 *Folio,* "Mr. William Shakespeare's Comedies, Histories, and Tragedies," accurately grouped *Julius Caesar* with *Macbeth, Hamlet,* and other tragedies. The ten plays presented as "histories" are exclusively concerned with kings of England: this is readily understandable for an English playwright writing exclusively for English audiences. But it is significant that, of the *Folio's* eleven tragedies, one is concerned with matters Greek, and four, or more than a third of the total, are based on the history of Rome. *Julius Caesar* is of course among this number.

Shakespeare's audience, and Shakespeare himself, were plainly much preoccupied with historical stories in general. The deep interest in matters Roman, however, was part of an abiding, far-reaching Renaissance concern—both in England and all across Europe—for what was still regarded as the mother and model of great states and lasting civilizations. Then, and for another more than three hundred years, Austria claimed to be an incarnation of the Holy Roman Empire. Just as Latin was without question the dominant language of intellectual discourse, as well as the basic subject of instruction in all but the most elementary of schools, so too Roman (and to a lesser extent Greek) mythology was, quite simply, the essential substance of "mythology." The names and something of the stories of Roman gods, and famous Roman men (and a few Roman women), were known to virtually everyone, whether or not literate or possessing any knowledge of Latin. "As for [Renaissance] theory and practice of historical writing," Douglas Bush observed drily, "it was the ancients who taught that."[1] George Puttenham's *The Arte of English Poesie* (1589) subtitles its second chapter even more revealingly: "That there may be an art of our English poesie, aswell [*sic*] as there is of the Latine and Greeke."[2]

Probably written in 1599, and first staged in that year, *Julius Caesar* is thus steeped in attitudes, in wide-ranging classical learning, and to a significant degree in rhetoric heavily derived from a long-dead civilization that, for many centuries, did not seem likely ever to truly die. It is not that Shakespeare deceives himself about the corruption and brutality underlying Roman life, just as they underlay that of Elizabethan England (and as, in all human societies, they are inevitably still fundamental). *Julius Caesar* is a relentlessly honest, profoundly moral portrait of the life of power, in which Shakespeare's characters freely deceive both each other and themselves.

Seven of those named on the list of characters are dead when the play ends. Six conspirators are as good as dead. And the two men who have triumphed, Octavius and Mark Antony, will before long fight each other in yet another deadly war, which Antony will not survive. All of those who die have plainly chosen (or will choose) their own fatal path. Many have been warned, and have multiple opportunities to reconsider; none do. If we label these determinedly death-oriented stances "stoic," we will be in good part correct, for Stoicism is indeed a set of beliefs central to the Roman way of life. Neither pain nor pleasure mattered a great deal, according to this strongly fatalistic viewpoint. And death, when at its own good time it chose to come, was neither avoidable nor worth avoiding. In those circumstances, one might as well welcome death and have it over with. Brutus and Cassius are suicides, and young Cato (like his own famous father) actively embraces death. All-powerful Julius Caesar, seeing that his belovèd Brutus is one of the assassins, first declares, "Et tu, Brute?" "And you too, Brutus?"—which is plainly not an interrogative but a rhetorical question. He then announces, "Then fall, Caesar," and dies. Could there be anything more stoical?

What makes the play a genuine tragedy is that the characters plainly possess the power and also the capacity for reasoned understanding, which could have spelled a different ending. So too was the ancient father of all tragic heroes, Oedipus, a quick-thinking, decisive, politically and militarily adept leader. He is not (or does not think he is) a king born but a king self-made. His reign is lauded and, for a time, highly successful. But human beings cannot avoid the consequences of who they are and what their essential nature leads or compels them to do. Julius Caesar conquered Britain, among other and often larger and more important regions. Indeed, he made himself ruler of the known world. And there is no iron law making it necessary for men so highly placed to die, violently and prematurely, at other men's hands. So far as is known, Genghis Khan died in his bed, as did Joseph Stalin.

Shakespeare gives us a Julius Caesar both magnificent and petty, at the same time commandingly powerful and yet open to flattery and deception. Not dramatically the dominant character in the play, he remains the linchpin around which the narrative turns. But what may well most distinguish Shakespeare's Julius Caesar from another of his most famous creations, Hamlet, is the consistent infusion into this, as into all the characters, of Roman-derived attitudes and Roman-like rhetoric.

> Cowards die many times before their deaths,
> The valiant never taste of death but once.
> Of all the wonders that I yet have heard,
> It seems to me most strange that men should fear,
> Seeing that death, a necessary end,
> Will come when it will come.

$$(2.2.32-37)$$

Caesar thus speaks to his wife, Calphurnia, who has begged him not to go to the Capitol, fearing dire consequences. Hamlet too contemplates death, but when his friend Horatio offers to arrange the cancelation of a fencing exercise (about which Hamlet has expressed strong misgivings), Hamlet responds:

> We defy augury. There's a special providence in the fall of a sparrow. If it be now, 'tis not to come. If it be not to come, it will be now. If it be not now, yet it will come. The readiness is all. Since no man, of aught he leaves, knows aught, what is't to leave betimes? Let be. (5.2.205–209)

The substance of what the two characters are saying is in essence the same: Why worry ourselves about when death will come? Further, though Hamlet's speech is cast in prose, and Caesar's in verse, the steady, even tone of Caesar's words is closer to what we think of as prose. Hamlet's words sparkle, leaping and jumping, turning and spinning, as we expect poetry to do.

Hamlet was written roughly two years later than *Julius Caesar,* so we cannot attribute these basic rhetorical differences to some major developmental change in Shakespeare. And in *Romeo and Juliet,* a play written some three or fours earlier than *Julius Caesar,* Shakespeare has presented us with a character, Romeo, contemplating his death:

> How oft when men are at the point of death
> Have they been merry! Which their keepers call
> A light'ning before death. O how may I
> Call this a light'ning?

> (5.3.88–91)

The sentiments, here, are dissimilar. But the rhetoric is almost incredibly more heightened. One can perhaps talk of Hamlet's remarks as having a Stoic link, though the emotional flavor is vastly un-Roman. But Romeo's words absolutely soar, as does the entire play of which he is the leading male figure. There is nothing Roman about him.

And we cannot attribute the sturdy, even flow of Julius Caesar's words to a Shakespearean decline, for he was soon to write *Othello, King Lear,* and *Macbeth.* Neither is Caesar the sole character to adopt Roman-like rhetoric. The play's major character is Brutus, and in both substance and rhetoric Shakespeare makes him equally decisively Roman. Just before he commits suicide, Brutus has the following brief exchange with Volumnius (a minor figure):

Brutus   Come hither, good Volumnius, list a word.
Volumnius   What says my lord?
Brutus   Why, this, Volumnius.

> The ghost of Caesar hath appeared to me
> Two several times by night. At Sardis, once,

And this last night, here in Philippi fields.

I know my hour is come.

Volumnius   Not so, my lord.

Brutus   Nay, I am sure it is, Volumnius.

Thou seest the world, Volumnius, how it goes.

Our enemies have beat us to the pit.

It is more worthy to leap in ourselves,

Than tarry till they push us. Good Volumnius,

Thou know'st that we two went to school together.

Even for that our love of old, I prithee

Hold thou my sword-hilts, whilst I run on it.

(5.5.13−27)

The utter (even if only outward) calm of "Nay, I am sure it is," or the apparently placid request to his old school companion to hold his sword while he throws himself on it, are stunningly Stoical. Brutus casts the longest shadow of anyone in the play, and not simply because, unlike Julius Caesar, he survives until the final act. Shakespeare deepens and extends the character until, in psychological complexity, Brutus stands beside the major figures in any of the plays. But from first to last, he remains a clearly identifiable Roman figure.

Shakespeare does not insist on the same rhetorical configuration in other plays involving Roman characters, not even when they are characters we have also seen in *Julius Caesar*. Mark Antony returns as the leading male figure in *Antony and Cleopatra,* probably written just after *King Lear* and *Macbeth*. In act 4, scene 14, having just been defeated in final battle with Octavius, he asks a subordinate, Eros, to kill him. When Eros kills himself, instead, Antony speaks the following:

                    Thrice-nobler than myself,
Thou teachest me, O valiant Eros, what
I should, and thou couldst not. My queen and Eros
Have by their brave instruction got upon me [succeeded in
achieving]
A nobleness in record. But I will be
A bridegroom in my death, and run into't
As to a lover's bed. Come then, and Eros,
Thy master dies thy scholar.

                                                    (lines 95–102)

How like Romeo Anthony seems, here! He is very, very different in *Julius Caesar,* as are all the characters in the earlier play.

This cannot be, nor is it, accidental. That Shakespeare was both a superbly successful playwright and, at the same time, a committed experimenter, at virtually every level of the dramatic art, is hardly a secret. Nor has this particular experiment gone unnoticed. More than sixty-five years ago, the poet-critic Mark Van Doren noted:

All of [*Julius Caesar's*] persons tend to talk alike; their
training has been forensic and therefore uniform, so that
they can say anything with both efficiency and ease. With
Marcellus' first speech in the opening scene the play
swings into its style: a style which will make it appear that
nobody experiences the least difficulty in saying what he
thinks. The phrasing is invariably flawless from the oral
point of view; the breathing is right; no thought is too
long for order or too short for roundness. Everything is
brilliantly and surely said; the effects are underlined, the
I's are firmly dotted. Speeches have tangible outline, like

plastic objects, and the drift from one of them to another has never to be guessed, for it is clearly stated.[3]

It is equally clear than Van Doren disapproves. As he goes on to say of a speech by Brutus, "This is fine, like everything else in *Julius Caesar,* but it is rotund and political." Van Doren believes, on what evidence I do not know, that "in such an atmosphere Caesar [and also Shakespeare] has little chance to be himself."[4] Another fine poet-critic, John Berryman, first observing that Shakespeare "was an unpredictable author," seems to me to have gotten things in a clearer perspective: "[In *Julius Caesar*] . . . a sobriety determines against any elevation of diction [i.e., rhetoric] more completely than in anything else he ever did . . . One might suppose this (and I do) a deliberately classical intention."[5] Rosalie Colie sees precisely the same thing: "By picking up hints from . . . the rhetoric books, Shakspeare could treat Brutus and Anthony as the living exemplars of what otherwise have been mere *topoi* [tropes, conventions]: he could make them live the styles in which they chose to speak."[6] Gert Ronberg speaks of Roman rhetoric, in the following comment, as exemplified, in Elizabethan England, by John Lyly's *Euphues* (1578–80): "Shakespeare was [not] averse to using a Euphuistic style when required. The pointing of antithesis and balancing of syntactic members are essentially features belonging to oratory. . . . [Unlike Lyly,] Shakespeare employs the style seriously in the situation to which he thinks it belongs, viz. in the Roman forum . . . [of] *Julius Caesar.*"[7]

And despite Van Doren's strictures, the play has from the start fascinated audiences. The distinguished twentieth-century actress Margaret Webster observes that "the dramatic quality of the play has made it eternally acceptable in the theatre. It shares with the greatest plays that spaciousness of conception which enables any one of twenty interpretations . . . Its protagonists remain themselves, but their pulse still beats through the civilized world."[8] Wrote John Weever, in 1601, "The many-headed multitude were drawn / By Brutus' speech, that Caesar was ambitious."[9] F. E. Halliday notes that "*Julius Caesar* was one of the three or four [Shakespearean] plays spared by 17th- and 18th-century improvers. At the Restoration it went to the King's company, who produced it in 1672. . . . It was often revived in the 18th century."[10] Writing in 1731 to England's Lord Bolingbroke, Voltaire reported: "With what pleasure did I not see in London your [that is, the English nation's] tragedy of *Julius Caesar,* which, for one hundred and fifty years, has been the delight of your nation!"[11] A Scandinavian scholar records that the influence of the play was felt by Sweden's greatest playwright, August Strindberg: "As the only major dramatist to devote as much attention to his nation's history as Shakespeare, Strindberg demands comparison to his English forebear. In fact, he insisted upon it. . . . Strindberg repeatedly proclaims himself a student and an admirer of Shakespeare. *Julius Caesar,* with its presentation of Caesar as 'merely a human being' ('endast en människa'), inspired the antiheroic stance of [Strindberg's] *Mäster Olof.*"[12]

Critics, too, have found the play deeply satisfying. Marion Trousdale, writing about rhetorical issues in Shakespeare, speaks of "the dramatic effectiveness of the method that was to reach its ultimate fullness in *Lear.*"[13] Rosalie Colie takes this a bit farther: "In *Julius Caesar,* Shakespeare dealt in the problems of politics . . . ; nothing is simple here—not even the rhetoric officially designated as 'plain.' . . . Among so much that he has done [in *Julius Caesar*], Shakespeare has here examined not only the motives of political men engaged by enormous power, but the problematics of public utterance as well, by means of which such motives were traditionally displayed—and concealed."[14] The classicist David Grene observes that "it is the mysterious nature of power, as sought for and exercised, that holds the center of the scene [in *Julius Caesar*]: how it corrupts and distorts the ethics of private life and the idealism of those who seek it. . . . For the leaders, then, the pattern becomes a baleful fate, impersonal as the gods in Sophocles. . . . It is in *Julius Caesar* that Shakespeare shows us a state where there is no system at all for the orderly succession of one power holder by another."[15]

The three plays Shakespeare wrote immediately after *Julius Caesar* were *As You Like It, Twelfth Night,* and *Hamlet.* Like the characters of *Julius Caesar,* we deceive only ourselves if we think the orderly march of both its narrative and its rhetoric signals a drama of little depth or mystery. It is never sensible, or even safe, for ordinary mortals to condescend to greatness.

Notes

1. Douglas Bush, *Prefaces to Renaissance Literature* (New York: W. W. Norton, 1965), 11.
2. G. Gregory Smith, ed., *Elizabethan Critical Essays,* 2 vols. (Oxford: Clarendon Press, 1904), 1:5.
3. Mark Van Doren, *Shakespeare* (New York: Holt, 1939), 153–154.
4. Van Doren, *Shakespeare,* 157.
5. John Berryman, *Berryman's Shakespeare,* edited by John Haffenden, preface by Robert Giroux (New York: Farrar, Straus and Giroux, 1999), 79.
6. Rosalie Colie, *Shakespeare's Living Art* (Princeton, N.J.: Princeton University Press, 1974), 171.
7. Gert Ronberg, *A Way with Words: The Language of English Renaissance Literature* (London: Arnold, 1992), 177.
8. Margaret Webster, *Shakespeare without Tears* (New York: Whittlesey House, 1942), 212.

9. Gamini Salgado, *Eyewitnesses of Shakespeare: First Hand Accounts of Performances, 1590–1890* (New York: Barnes and Noble, 1975), 22.

10. F. E. Halliday, *A Shakespeare Companion, 1564–1964,* rev. ed. (Harmondsworth: Penguin, 1964), 261.

11. Oswald Le Winter, ed. *Shakespeare in Europe* (Cleveland, Ohio: Meridian, 1963), 34.

12. Matthew H. Wikander, *The Play of Truth and State: Historical Drama from Shakespeare to Brecht* (Baltimore: Johns Hopkins University Press, 1986), 161.

13. Marion Trousdale, *Shakespeare and the Rhetoricians* (Chapel Hill: University of North Carolina Press, 1982), 135.

14. Colie, *Shakespeare's Living Art,* 175.

15. David Grene, *The Actor in History: A Study in Shakespearean Stage Poetry* (University Park: Pennsylvania State University Press, 1988), 85, 92.

SOME ESSENTIALS OF THE
SHAKESPEAREAN STAGE

The Stage

- There was no *scenery* (backdrops, flats, and so on).

- Compared to today's elaborate, high-tech productions, the Elizabethan stage had few *on-stage* props. These were mostly handheld: a sword or dagger, a torch or candle, a cup or flask. Larger props, such as furniture, were used sparingly.

- Costumes (some of which were upper-class castoffs, belonging to the individual actors) were elaborate. As in most premodern and very hierarchical societies, clothing was the distinctive mark of who and what a person was.

- What the actors *spoke,* accordingly, contained both the dramatic and narrative material we have come to expect in a theater (or movie house) and (1) the setting, including details of the time of day, the weather, and so on, and (2) the occasion. The *dramaturgy* is thus very different from that of our own time, requiring much more attention to verbal and gestural matters. Strict realism was neither intended nor, under the circumstances, possible.

- There was *no curtain.* Actors entered and left via doors in the back of the stage, behind which was the "tiring-room," where actors put on or changed their costumes.

- In *public theaters* (which were open-air structures), there was no *lighting;* performances could take place only in daylight hours.

- For *private* theaters, located in large halls of aristocratic houses, candlelight illumination was possible.

The Actors

- Actors worked in *professional,* for-profit companies, sometimes organized and owned by other actors, and sometimes by entrepreneurs who could afford to erect or rent the company's building. Public theaters could hold, on average, two thousand playgoers, most of whom viewed and listened while standing. Significant profits could be and were made. Private theaters were smaller, more exclusive.

- There was *no director.* A book-holder/prompter/props manager, standing in the tiring-room behind the backstage doors, worked from a text marked with entrances and exits and notations of any special effects required for that particular script. A few such books have survived. Actors had texts only of their own parts, speeches being cued to a few prior words. There were few and often no rehearsals, in our modern use of the term, though there was often some coaching of individuals. Since Shakespeare's England was largely an oral culture, actors learned their parts rapidly and retained them for years. This was *repertory* theater, repeating popular plays and introducing some new ones each season.

- *Women* were not permitted on the professional stage. Most female roles were acted by *boys;* elderly women were played by grown men.

The Audience

- London's professional theater operated in what might be called a "red-light" district, featuring brothels, restaurants, and the kind of *open-air entertainment* then most popular, like bear-baiting (in which a bear, tied to a stake, was set on by dogs).

- A theater audience, like most of the population of Shakespeare's England, was largely made up of *illiterates.* Being able to read and write, however, had nothing to do with intelligence or concern with language, narrative, and characterization. People attracted to the theater tended to be both extremely verbal and extremely volatile. Actors were sometimes attacked, when the audience was dissatisfied; quarrels and fights were relatively common. Women were regularly in attendance, though no reliable statistics exist.

- Drama did not have the cultural esteem it has in our time, and plays were not regularly printed. Shakespeare's often appeared in book form, but not with any supervision or other involvement on his part. He wrote a good deal of nondramatic poetry as well, yet so far as we know he did not authorize or supervise *any* work of his that appeared in print during his lifetime.

- Playgoers, who had paid good money to see and hear, plainly gave dramatic performances careful, detailed attention. For some closer examination of such matters, see Burton Raffel, "Who Heard the Rhymes and How: Shakespeare's Dramaturgical Signals," *Oral Tradition* 11 (October 1996): 190–221, and Raffel, "Metrical Dramaturgy in Shakespeare's Earlier Plays," *CEA Critic* 57 (Spring–Summer 1995): 51–65.

Julius Caesar

CHARACTERS (DRAMATIS PERSONAE)

Julius Caesar

Marcus Brutus

Caius Cassius (Brutus' brother-in-law)

Casca

Octavius Caesar (great-nephew of Julius Caesar)

Mark Antony

Lepidus

Cicero, Publius, Popilius Lena (senators)

Marullus, Flavius (tribunes)

Cinna, Caius Ligarius, Metellus Cimber, Decius Brutus, Trebonius
(conspirators)

Calphurnia (Caesar's wife)

Portia (Brutus' wife)

Lucius (Brutus' personal servant)

Titinius (Caesar's personal servant)

Lucilius, Pindarus, Messala, Young Cato, Strato (officers in army of
Brutus and Cassius)

Varro, Claudio, Clitus, Dardanius, Volumnius (soldiers in army of
Brutus and Cassius), *Artemidorus, Carpenter, Cobbler, Soothsayer,
Cinna* (a poet – neither a conspirator nor a lucky man), and
another Poet (Marcus Favonius, though not named in the text)

Servants, Messengers, Plebeians

Caesar's Ghost

Act I

SCENE I

Rome, a street

ENTER FLAVIUS, MARULLUS, AND COMMONERS

Flavius   Hence! Home, you idle[1] creatures, get you home.

Is this a holiday? What, know you not

(Being mechanical)[2] you ought not walk

Upon a laboring day without the sign[3]

Of your profession? Speak, what trade art thou?   5

Commoner 1 Why sir, a carpenter.[4]

Marullus   Where is thy leather apron and thy rule?[5]

What dost thou with thy best apparel on?

You sir, what trade are you?

---

1 (1) foolish, useless, worthless, (2) loafing
2 craftsmen
3 mark, symbol
4 carpenters did heavy, construction-type woodworking; joiners did small, finer, cabinetmaker-type woodworking
5 yardstick

10   *Commoner 2*   Truly, sir, in respect of[6] a fine[7] workman, I am but
      − as you would say − a cobbler.

      Marullus   But what trade[8] art thou? Answer me directly.[9]

      Commoner 2   A trade sir, that I hope I may use with a safe
      conscience, which is indeed, sir, a mender of bad soles.

15   *Flavius*   What trade, thou knave?[10] Thou naughty[11] knave,
      what trade?

      Commoner 2   Nay, I beseech you, sir, be not out[12] with me. Yet, if
      you be out,[13] sir, I can mend[14] you.

      Marullus   What meanest thou by that? Mend me, thou saucy

20   fellow?[15]

      Commoner 2   Why sir, cobble you.

      Flavius   Thou art a cobbler, art thou?

      Commoner 2   Truly, sir, all that I live by is with the awl.[16] I
      meddle with no tradesman's[17] matters, nor women's matters,

25   but with awl[18] I am indeed, sir, a surgeon[19] to old shoes.
      When they are in great danger, I recover[20] them. As proper[21]

handwritten: comparing to a good workman

handwritten margin: Not good

handwritten: Shakespeare is name punny

handwritten: a very idiot

handwritten: Eww be like a hat or like a sprite

handwritten: but of the joke

handwritten: angry or warn out

handwritten: oh, burn!

handwritten: this is the hook / comic relief

6 in respect of = with reference/in comparison to
7 highly accomplished, skilled, superior
8 way of life, employment
9 (1) straightforwardly, plainly, (2) correctly
10 rogue★
11 (1) wicked, (2) disobedient
12 put out, angry
13 i.e., out at the heels/soles
14 (1) repair, fix, (2) reform, improve
15 saucy fellow = insolent/presumptuous/rude★ person (negative)★
16 tool used for piercing leather (homonym of "all"); there is a sexual overtone,
    since "awl" = penis
17 other tradesman's
18 pun on "withal"
19 medical man, physician
20 (1) restore them to good health, (2) cover them again (with good leather)
21 good, worthy, of high quality

[handwritten: Flavius / Marullus R mundo rvo ftu Juke]

men as ever trod upon neat's[22] leather have gone[23] upon my
handiwork.

Flavius   But wherefore[24] art not in thy shop today?
Why dost thou lead these men about the streets?   30

Commoner 2 Truly, sir, to wear out their shoes, to get myself into
more work. But indeed, sir, we make holiday, to see Caesar
and to rejoice in his triumph.[25] *[handwritten: he really just wants $ and they want to see caesar]*

Marullus   Wherefore rejoice? What conquest brings he
home?
What tributaries[26] follow him to Rome,   *[handwritten: they want to see the captives walk thro on the streets of rome]*   35
To grace[27] in captive[28] bonds his chariot wheels?
You blocks,[29] you stones, you worse than senseless[30] things!
O you hard hearts, you cruel men of Rome,
Knew you not Pompey?[31] Many a time and oft[32]   *[handwritten: hes a good teacher]*
Have you climbed up to walls and battlements,[33]   40
To towers and windows, yea, to chimney tops,
Your infants in your arms, and there have sat
The livelong[34] day, with patient expectation,
To see great Pompey pass[35] the streets of Rome.

[handwritten margin note: In the past, the climb to see the pass's Great Pompey]

22 cattle: ox, cow, bull
23 walked
24 why   *[handwritten: Pompey has been defeated they shifted loyalty easily]*
25 Roman victory parade*
26 defeated enemies (who pay tax/tribute to their conquerors)
27 honor, adorn*
28 prisoner's
29 of solid wood
30 unable to use their senses
31 Roman leader defeated by Caesar
32 many = quantity; oft = frequency
33 indented parapets on top of walls (have YOU climbed UP to WALLS and
   BATtleMENTS)
34 whole long
35 go along

45 And when you saw his chariot but[36] appear,
Have you not made an universal[37] shout,
That[38] Tiber[39] trembled underneath her banks
To hear the replication[40] of your sounds
Made in her concave[41] shores?

50 And do you now put on your best attire?
And do you now cull[42] out a holiday?
And do you now strew flowers in his way,
That[43] comes in triumph over Pompey's blood?
Be gone!

55 Run to your houses, fall upon your knees,
Pray to the gods to intermit[44] the plague
That needs[45] must light[46] on this ingratitude.

Flavius Go, go, good countrymen, and for this fault[47]
Assemble all the poor men of your sort.[48]

60 Draw them to Tiber banks, and weep your tears
Into the channel,[49] till the lowest stream
Do kiss the most exalted[50] shores of all.[51]

---

36 just, barely, only
37 i.e., participated in by everyone
38 so that
39 river flowing through Rome into the Mediterranean
40 echo, reverberation
41 curved like inside of a circle (convex = curved like outside of a circle)
42 pluck, pick, select
43 he who
44 suspend, omit
45 necessarily
46 descend
47 defect, failing, wrong★
48 kind, rank, class
49 running water ("river")
50 elevated (in the sense of physical height)
51 i.e., until the aggregate of your tears causes the river to swell to its highest level

EXEUNT[52] COMMONERS

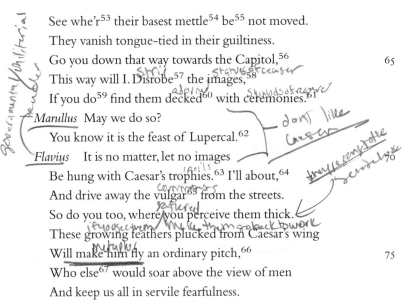

See whe'r[53] their basest mettle[54] be[55] not moved.

They vanish tongue-tied in their guiltiness.

Go you down that way towards the Capitol,[56]   65

This way will I. Disrobe[57] the images,[58]

If you do[59] find them decked[60] with ceremonies.[61]

Marullus May we do so?

You know it is the feast of Lupercal.[62]

Flavius It is no matter, let no images

Be hung with Caesar's trophies.[63] I'll about,[64]   70

And drive away the vulgar[65] from the streets.

So do you too, where you perceive them thick.

These growing feathers plucked from Caesar's wing

Will make him fly an ordinary pitch,[66]   75

Who else[67] would soar above the view of men

And keep us all in servile fearfulness.

EXEUNT

52 plural of "exit"

53 whether

54 basest metal = lowest, most unworthy/menial/inferior★ character, disposition, temperament, spirit ★

55 is ("be": subjunctive)

56 towering Roman temple dedicated to Jupiter

57 strip

58 statues of Caesar

59 used as an intensifier, often without additional/separate meaning★

60 adorned, covered

61 symbols of regard (flowers, scarves, crowns)

62 fertility festival, celebrated on 15 February (Lupercal: rural deity associated with Faunus/Pan)★

63 spoils, booty

64 go around

65 commoners (uneducated, ignorant)

66 ordinary pitch = regular/usual height

67 otherwise★

7

SCENE 2

A public place

FLOURISH[1] — *fanfare! indicates the importance of someone*

ENTER CAESAR, ANTONY (STRIPPED DOWN FOR MAKING
THE RELIGIOUS RUN), CALPHURNIA, PORTIA, DECIUS
BRUTUS, CICERO, BRUTUS, CASSIUS, AND CASCA,[2]
A CROWD AND A SOOTHSAYER[3] FOLLOWING

In the crowd

Caesar   Calphurnia!

Casca   Peace,[4] ho! Caesar speaks.

Caesar   Calphurnia![5]

Calphurnia Here my lord.[6]

Caesar   Stand you directly in Antonio's way,   *Antony is going on a run for fertility*

When he doth run his course.[7] Antonio!

5 *Antony*   Caesar, my lord?

Caesar   Forget not in your speed, Antonio,

To touch Calphurnia. For our elders say

The barren, touchèd in this holy chase,

Shake off their sterile curse.

Antony — loyal   I shall remember:

10   When Caesar says "Do this," it is performed.

Caesar   Set on, and leave no ceremony[8] out.

Caesar's son is adopted, Calphurnia is steril

1 fanfare (brass instruments)★
2 KAska
3 someone capable of predicting the future
4 silence, be quiet★ (the crowd is noisy)
5 the first three lines are metrically/prosodically counted as one complete
  iambic pentameter line: calFURnya PEACE ho CAESar SPEAKS
  calFURnya
6 husband (male head/lord of the household)
7 path★ (of the run/race)
8 rite, observance

FLOURISH

Soothsayer	Caesar!
Caesar	Ha? Who calls?
Casca	Bid every noise be still! Peace yet again!— shut up
Caesar	Who is it in the press[9] that calls on me?

I hear a tongue shriller than all the music

Cry "Caesar!" Speak. Caesar is[10] turned to hear.

Soothsayer	Beware the Ides[11] of March.[12]
Caesar	What man[13] is that?
Brutus	A soothsayer bids you beware the Ides of March.
Caesar	Set him before me, let me see his face.
Cassius	Fellow, come from the <u>throng</u>, look upon[14] Caesar.

crowd

Caesar	What say'st thou to me now? Speak once again.
Soothsayer	Beware the Ides of March— March 15
Caesar	He is a dreamer,[15] let us leave him. Pass.[16]

they think he's crazy

FLOURISH

EXEUNT ALL EXCEPT <u>BRUTUS</u> AND <u>CASSIUS</u>

they stay

Cassius	Will you go see the order[17] of the course?
Brutus	Not I.
Cassius	I pray you, do.

15

20

25

9 multitude, crowd★
10 has
11 EYEDZ
12 15 March (i.e., in exactly another month)
13 what man = who
14 at
15 visionary, having visions in his sleep
16 let us proceed
17 ranking, sequence

"Are you going to see the orders of the course"

Brutus   I am not ~~gamesome~~. [18] I do lack some part [19]   *playful*

Of that quick spirit [20] that is in Antony.

(I'm not enthusiastic)

30   Let me not hinder, Cassius, your desires.

being vague   I'll leave you.   *If you want to watch it, go ahead*

I've been watching you lately

Cassius   Brutus, I do observe [21] you now of late.

I have not [22] from your eyes that gentleness [23]   *observing your lack of emotion*

And show [24] of love as I was wont [25] to have.

35   You bear [26] too stubborn and too strange [27] a hand   *You've been distant*

* Napi? *

Over [28] your friend that loves you.   *you're sad*

Brutus   Cassius,

Don't be tricked   Be not deceived. If I have veiled my look,   *I have changed*

I turn the trouble [29] of my countenance [30]

Merely upon myself. Vexed I am

I'm troubled about new feelings

40   Of late with passions [31] of some difference, [32]

oh yeah, yaay!   Conceptions [33] only proper to [34] myself,

man vs. self conflict

18 sportive, playful, merry
19 portion, share★
20 quick spirit = lively ("full of life")★ (1) soul, essence, nature, character,★ (2) inclination, impulse
21 pay attention to
22 have not = have not experienced/felt
23 affability
24 display, demonstration, appearance★
25 accustomed
26 bear . . . a hand = treat, deal with (idiom from horsemanship)
27 stubborn . . . strange = inflexible, hard, fierce . . . unfamiliar, unusual, surprising
28 on, upon
29 disturbance, vexation, grief, perplexity
30 (1) appearance, face, (2) behavior
31 (1) feelings, emotions,★ (2) sufferings
32 diversity, dissimilarity
33 ideas, views
34 proper to = belonging/related to

this basically changes my behavior

Which give some soil[35] (perhaps) to my behaviors.[36]

But let not therefore my good friends be grieved –

Among which number, Cassius, be you[37] one – *Don't worry*

Nor construe[38] any further my neglect   45

Than that poor Brutus, with himself at war, *such emotional upheaval*

Forgets the shows of love to other men. – *he forgets to love*

Cassius Then Brutus, I have much mistook your passion, *he overanalyzed it all*

By means whereof[39] this breast of mine hath buried[40]

Thoughts of great value, worthy cogitations.   50

Tell me, good Brutus, can you see your face? *trick question*

Brutus No, Cassius. For the eye sees not itself

But[41] by reflection, by some other things.[42] *mirror*

Cassius 'Tis just,[43] *makes sense*

And it is very much lamented, Brutus,   55

That you have no such mirrors as will turn

Your hidden worthiness into[44] your eye, *no one is telling you how amazing you are*

That[45] you might see your shadow.[46] I have heard,

Where many of the best respect[47] in Rome

(Except immortal Caesar), speaking of Brutus   60

– says it aside to *they're modeling Caesar*
adds a point to their audience

35 stain, discoloration, tarnish

36 singular and plural were not, in Shakespeare's time, as sharply distinguished
as they are today

37 be you = you are

38 analyze, explain, interpret★

39 by means whereof = because of which mistake

40 hidden, concealed

41 except

42 other things = things different from itself

43 fair, honorable, correct

44 inTO

45 so that

46 your shadow = the image you cast / reveal to others (of yourself)

47 best respect = most respected / honored

And groaning underneath this age's yoke,[48] *era*

Have wished that noble Brutus had his eyes.

Brutus   Into what dangers would you[49] lead me, Cassius,

That you would have me seek into myself

65   For that which is not in me?

Cassius   Therefore good Brutus, be prepared to hear;

leading Brutus   And since you know you cannot see yourself

on, tricking   So well as by reflection, I, your glass,[50] *I will praise you*

him

he uses an   Will modestly discover[51] to yourself

ulterior motive

70   That of yourself which you yet know not of.

they're trying   And be not jealous on[52] me, gentle[53] Brutus,   *suspicious*

get to Brutus   Were I[54] a common laughter,[55] or did use[56]

To stale[57] with ordinary[58] oaths my love   *If I say this to everyone,*

To every new protester.[59] If you know   *then you should be weary*

of me. But I don't, so

75   That I do fawn on men and hug them hard   *you shouldn't*

And after scandal[60] them, or if you know

That I profess myself in[61] banqueting[62]

---

48 age's yoke = time/era's★ device for coupling draught animals together, so that they may pull as one★

49 would you = do you wish

50 mirror★

51 modestly discover = without exaggeration disclose/reveal★

52 jealous on = suspicious★ of

53 well-born, distinguished, excellent, gentlemanly★

54 were I = as if I were

55 person habitually laughed at/scorned (common = general, universal)★

56 did use = was in the habit of★

57 to stale = diminishing (Shakespeare often uses an infinitive where, today, we would use a participial)

58 everyday, regular, abundant

59 person making strong affirmations/claims

60 after scandal = afterwards slander

61 profess myself in = make a habit of

62 providing banquets for

To all the rout,[63] then hold me dangerous.

Brutus   What means this shouting? I do fear the people

Choose Caesar for their king.

Cassius   Ay, do you fear it?   80

Then must I think you would not have it so.

Brutus   I would not, Cassius, yet I love him well.

But wherefore do you hold me here so long?

What is it that you would impart to me?

If it be aught toward the general[64] good,   85

Set honor in one eye, and death i'the other,

And I will look on both indifferently.[65]

For let the gods so speed me[66] as[67] I love

The name of honor more than I fear death.

Cassius   I know that virtue to be in you, Brutus,   90

As well as I do know your outward favor.[68]

Well, honor is the subject of my story.

I cannot tell what you and other men

Think of this life. But for my single[69] self,

I had as lief[70] not be as live to be   95

In awe of such a thing as I myself.

I was born free as Caesar, so were you.

63 mob, herd
64 common, universal*
65 without distinction, equally
66 speed me = make me successful*
67 to the degree/extent that
68 appearance, look*
69 individual, solitary
70 had as lief = would be as glad/willing

They're just as good as Caeser

We both have fed as well,[71] and we can both

Endure the winter's cold as well as he.

100 For once, upon a raw and gusty day, *why is Caesar so special*

The troubled[72] Tiber chafing with[73] her shores, *personification*

Caesar said to me, "Dar'st thou, Cassius, now

I dare you to swim across the river

Leap in with me into this angry flood,[74] *in the winter*

And swim to yonder point?" Upon the word,

105 Accoutred[75] as I was, I plungèd in

And bade him follow. So indeed he did. *they both did*

The torrent[76] roared, and we did buffet[77] it

With lusty sinews,[78] throwing it aside

And stemming[79] it with hearts of controversy.[80]

110 But ere we could arrive the point proposed,

Caesar cried, "Help me, Cassius, or I sink!"

I, as[81] Aeneas,[82] our great ancestor, *will drown*

Did from the flames of Troy upon his shoulder *Cassius had to*

simile The old Anchises[83] bear, so from the waves of Tiber *carry Caeser to shore*

115 Did I[84] the tired Caesar. And this man

Is[85] now become a god, and Cassius is *now*

71 fed as well = eaten as well as Caesar has
72 agitated, stormy
73 chafing with = fretting/rubbing/angry at
74 river
75 dressed
76 rushing stream
77 strike, beat, fight with
78 lusty sinews = lively/vigorous muscles
79 making headway ("swimming")
80 of controversy = competing/competitive
81 just as
82 founder of Rome (anEEus)
83 Aeneas' father (anKEEzeez)
84 did I = did I bear
85 has

A wretched creature and must bend his body[86]   *I saved him and he*
    is at the same levels
  If Caesar carelessly but nod on him.

Jealous   He had a fever when he was in Spain,

angry   And when the fit was on him I did mark   *weak/hurting*   120

  How he did shake. 'Tis true, this god did shake.   *a seizure*

  His coward[87] lips did from their color fly,

  And that same eye whose bend[88] doth awe the world

  Did lose his[89] luster. I did hear him groan.

  Ay, and that tongue of his that bade the Romans   125

  Mark him, and write his speeches in their books,

  Alas, it cried, "Give me some drink, Titinius,"   *Similie*

  As[90] a sick girl. Ye gods, it doth amaze me   *weak, sick men*

  A man of such a feeble temper should

  So get the start of[91] the majestic world   130

  And bear the palm[92] alone.   *symbol of victory*

SHOUT. FLOURISH

Brutus   Another general shout?   *his setting*

  I do believe that these applauses[93] are

  For some new honors that are heaped on Caesar.

Cassius   Why man, he doth bestride[94] the narrow[95] world   135

---

86 bend his body = bow
87 (figurative: the fearful/frightened lips run from their own natural color)
88 glance
89 its
90 like, just as
91 start of = jump on
92 symbol of triumph/victory
93 acclamations, demonstrations of loud approval
94 sit with legs astride, as on a horse
95 small, confined, limited

Like a colossus,[96] and we petty men
Walk under his huge legs and peep about
To[97] find ourselves dishonorable graves.
Men at some time are masters of their fates.
140   The fault (dear Brutus) is not in our stars,[98]
But in ourselves, that we are underlings.
Brutus and Caesar: what should[99] be in that "Caesar"?
Why should that name be sounded[100] more than yours?
Write them together, yours is as fair[101] a name.
145   Sound them, it doth become the mouth as well.
Weigh them, it is as heavy. Conjure[102] with 'em,
Brutus will start[103] a spirit as soon as Caesar.
Now in the names of all the gods at once,
Upon what meat[104] doth this our Caesar feed,
150   That he is grown so great? Age, thou art shamed!
Rome, thou hast lost the breed[105] of noble bloods!
When went there by an age,[106] since the great flood,
But it was famed with more than with one man?
When could they say (till now), that talked of Rome,
155   That her wide walks[107] encompassed[108] but one man?

96 huge statue of a man (the ancient colossus at Rhodes, island in Aegean Sea,
    off Turkey, was said to be 75 feet tall, and to "bestride" the harbor)
97 in order to
98 i.e., astrologically determined destinies
99 must
100 proclaimed, uttered
101 beautiful, desirable, elegant★
102 call up supernatural beings★
103 bring/jump/burst up
104 food
105 parentage, lineage
106 when went there by an age = when did an age go by
107 pathways★
108 surrounded, encircled, contained

It wasn't just one man who started it,
why is there just one man now

Now is it Rome indeed,[109] and room[110] enough,

When there is in it but one only man.

O! You and I have heard our fathers say

There was a Brutus[111] once that would have brooked[112]

Th' eternal Divel[113] *devil* to keep his state[114] in Rome   160

As easily as a king.[115]

Brutus That you do *in fact* love me,[116] I am nothing jealous.   *I understand and*
we should do something

What you would work me to,[117] I have some aim.[118]   *But wait til the*

How[119] I have thought of this, and of these times,   *I'll think it over*
and well tell

I shall recount[120] hereafter. For this present,[121]   *again*   165

I would[122] not so[123] (with love I might entreat you)

Be any further moved.[124] What you have said

I will consider. What you have to say

I will with patience hear, and find a time

Both meet[125] to hear and answer[126] such high things.   170

---

109 truly, really

110 space ("Rome" and "room" were homonyms)

111 Lucius Junius Brutus, founder of the Roman Republic, ca. 519 B.C. (*brutus*
      = moron, idiot, a pose that the ancient Brutus used to avoid assassination
      by Tarquin, then king of Rome)

112 put up with, tolerated

113 Devil

114 his state = the Devil's (1) existence / life, (2) rule

115 as easily as a king = just as readily as he (Brutus) would have tolerated a
      Roman king

116 in fact

117 toward

118 guess, conjecture

119 what

120 tell, narrate

121 this present = now

122 wish, want, desire

123 thus

124 impelled, put in motion

125 proper, appropriate★

126 respond to★

Till then, my noble friend, chew upon this.
Brutus had rather be a villager[127]
Than to repute[128] himself a son of Rome
Under these[129] hard conditions as this time
175   Is like[130] to lay upon us.

his words were very strong and influential

Cassius I am glad that my weak words
Have struck but thus much show of fire from Brutus.

ENTER CAESAR AND HIS FOLLOWERS

Brutus   The games are done and Caesar is returning.
Cassius As they pass by, pluck Casca by the sleeve,
180   And he will (after his sour fashion)[131] tell you

what important say

What hath proceeded[132] worthy note[133] today.
Brutus   I will do so. But look you, Cassius,
The angry spot[134] doth glow on Caesar's brow,
And all the rest look like a chidden train.[135]
185   Calphurnia's cheek is pale, and Cicero[136]
Looks with such ferret[137] and such fiery eyes
As we have seen him in the Capitol,
Being crossed[138] in conference by some senators.

the people are angry and sickly and pissed. Probably shit wine down.

127 i.e., a dweller in the countryside and not a citizen of *the* city in the world,
    Rome
128 consider, think
129 such
130 likely
131 style, habit, manner★
132 happened, taken place
133 of note
134 mark, stain
135 chidden train = scolded/reproved★ retinue/following
136 SIseROW
137 polecat
138 crossed in conference = thwarted/opposed★ in discussion/debate

Cassius Casca will tell us what the matter is.

CASSIUS AND BRUTUS STAND ASIDE

Caesar Antonio.   190

Antony Caesar?

Caesar Let me have men about me that are[139] fat,   ) *he wants to surround*
    Sleek-headed men[140] and such as sleep o' nights.   ) *himself with sheep*
    Yond Cassius has a lean and hungry look,
    He thinks too much. Such men are dangerous.   *he is weary of*
                                                                Cassius   195

Antony Fear him not, Caesar, he's not dangerous.   *los*
    He is a noble Roman, and well given.[141]

Caesar Would he were fatter. But I fear him not.
    Yet if my name[142] were liable[143] to fear,
    I do not know the man I should avoid   200
    So soon as that spare[144] Cassius. He reads much,
    He is a great observer, and he looks
    Quite through[145] the deeds of men. He loves no plays,[146]
    As thou dost, Antony. He hears[147] no music.   *he is a great observer*
    Seldom he smiles, and smiles in such a sort   *and is dubious and doubt*
                                                                  and may overthrow   205
    As if he mocked himself and scorned his spirit   *Caesar*
    That[148] could be moved to smile at anything.
    Such men as he be never at heart's ease

---

139 that are = men that are
140 sleek-headed men = men with smooth heads of hair
141 disposed, inclined
142 family name, lineage
143 amenable, likely
144 thin, lean
145 looks quite through = very exhaustively / wholly penetrates / searches
146 exercise, sports
147 listens to
148 scorned his spirit that = found it ludicrous / contemptible that his spirit

Whiles they behold a greater[149] than themselves,

210 And therefore are they very dangerous.

I rather[150] tell thee what is to be feared

Than what I fear, for always I am Caesar.

Come on my right hand, for this ear is deaf,

And tell me truly what thou think'st of him.

EXEUNT CAESAR AND ALL HIS FOLLOWERS, EXCEPT CASCA

215 *Casca* You pulled me by the cloak. Would you[151] speak with
me?

Brutus Ay Casca, tell us what hath chanced[152] today
That Caesar looks so sad.[153]

Casca Why, you were with him, were you not?

220 *Brutus* I should[154] not then ask Casca what had chanced.

Casca Why, there was a crown offered him, and being offered
him, he put it by[155] with the back of his hand, thus, and then
the people fell a-shouting.

Brutus What was the second noise for?

225 *Casca* Why, for that too.

Cassius They shouted thrice. What was the last cry for?

Casca Why, for that too.

Brutus Was the crown offered him thrice?

Casca Ay marry was't, and he put it by thrice, every time

---

149 greater man
150 more readily
151 would you = do you wish to
152 happened, occurred*
153 serious, somber*
154 would
155 put it by = thrust it aside ("rejected it")

gentler[156] than other, and at every putting-by mine honest   230
neighbors[157] shouted.

Cassius Who offered him the crown?

Casca Why, Antony.

Brutus Tell us the manner of it, gentle Casca.

Casca I can as well be hanged as tell the manner of it. It was   235
mere foolery; I did not mark it. I saw Mark Antony offer him
a crown, yet 'twas not a crown neither, 'twas one of these
coronets.[158] And as I told you, he put it by once. But for all
that, to my thinking, he would fain[159] have had it. Then he[160]
offered it to him again. Then he put it by again. But to my   240
thinking, he was very loath to lay his fingers off it. And then
he offered it the third time. He put it the third time by, and
still as he refused it, the rabblement[161] hooted and clapped
their chapped[162] hands and threw up their sweaty
nightcaps[163] and uttered such a deal[164] of stinking breath,   245
because Caesar refused the crown, that it had almost choked
Caesar. For he swounded[165] and fell down at it. And for mine
own part, I durst not laugh, for fear of opening my lips and
receiving[166] the bad air.

Cassius But soft, I pray you. What, did Caesar swound?   250

---

156 more courteously/politely/softly
157 honest neighbors = respectable/honorable★ people standing next to me
158 small/lesser crowns
159 be glad/wanted to
160 Antony
161 rabble, crowd, mob
162 cracked (i.e., workingmen's hands)
163 universally worn by both sexes
164 quantity, lot
165 swooned, fainted
166 taking in

Casca is kind of an idiot

Casca   He fell down in the marketplace, and foamed at mouth, and was speechless.

he has epilepsy

Brutus   'Tis very like.[167] He hath the falling sickness.[168]

Cassius   No, Caesar hath it not, but you and I,

255   And honest Casca, we have the falling sickness.[169]

Casca   I know not what you mean by that, but I am sure Caesar fell down. If the tag-rag[170] people did not clap him, and hiss him, according as he pleased and displeased them, as they use to do the players in the theater, I am no true[171] man.

260   **Brutus**   What said he when he came unto himself?

what did he say when he woke up

Casca   Marry, before he fell down, when he perceived the common herd was glad he refused the crown, he plucked me ope[172] his doublet[173] and offered them his throat to cut.

perhaps he wants the crown, but really doesn't want to accept it.

he wanted the people to kill him

An[174] I had been a man of any occupation,[175] if I would not have taken him at a word,[176] I would I might go to hell among the rogues. And so he fell. When he came to himself

265

perhaps he doesn't want the crown

again, he said if he had done or said anything amiss,[177] he desired their worships[178] to think it was his infirmity. Three or four wenches,[179] where I stood, cried "Alas, good soul!"

It was the sickness so I take it back

167 probable, likely
168 falling sickness = epilepsy
169 WE have the FALling SICKness
170 tag-rag = rabble ("dressed in tags [hanging/torn bits of clothing] and rags")
171 honest, upright
172 plucked me ope = opened
173 close-fitting, jacket-like garment
174 if
175 any occupation = any trade ("a tradesman/mechanical")
176 at a word = right away, as soon as he had spoken
177 faulty, wrong, inappropriate★ (i.e., while he was in his fit)
178 honors (form of address to men of rank/distinction)
179 young women

yes they will want [handwritten]

and forgave him with all their hearts. But there's no heed[180]   270
to be taken of them. If Caesar had stabbed their mothers, they
would have done no less. *Caesar could have gotten away* [handwritten]

Brutus   And after that, he came, thus sad away?   *with everything* [handwritten]

Casca   Ay.

Cassius   Did Cicero say anything?   275

Casca   Ay, he spoke Greek.

Cassius   To what effect?

Casca   Nay, an I tell you that, I'll ne'er look you i' the face
again.[181] But those that understood him smiled at one
another and shook their heads. But for mine own part, it was   280
Greek to me. I could tell you more news too. Marullus and
Flavius, for pulling scarfs off Caesar's images, are put to   *were they killed?* [handwritten]
silence.[182] Fare you well. There was more foolery yet, if I   *Neither were dismissed from office* [handwritten]
could remember it.

Cassius   Will you sup[183] with me tonight, Casca?   285

Casca   No, I am promised forth.[184]

Cassius   Will you dine with me tomorrow?

Casca   Ay, if I be alive and your mind hold[185] and your dinner
worth the eating.

Cassius   Good. I will expect you.   290

Casca   Do so. Farewell both.

EXIT CASCA

180 attention, notice
181 i.e., he would not be able to face Cassius, being too ashamed for having
      lied, if he had pretended he had in fact understood
182 put to silence = (?) (1) dismissed from office, *or* (2) executed
183 dine, have supper
184 promised forth = engaged elsewhere ("away")
185 remain the same / constant ("not change")

Brutus   What a blunt[186] fellow is this grown to be!
   He was quick mettle when he went to school.
Cassius   So is he now in execution[187]
295   Of any bold or noble enterprise,[188]
   However[189] he puts on[190] this tardy form.[191]
   This rudeness[192] is a sauce to his good wit,[193]
   Which gives men stomach[194] to digest his words
   With better appetite.
300 *Brutus*   And so it is.[195] For this time I will leave you.
   Tomorrow, if you please to speak with me,
   I will come home to you. Or if you will,
   Come home to me, and I will wait for you.
Cassius   I will do so. Till then, think of the world.[196]

EXIT BRUTUS

305   Well Brutus, thou art noble. Yet I see
   Thy honorable mettle may be wrought[197]
   From that[198] it is disposed. Therefore it is meet
   That noble minds keep[199] ever with their likes,[200]

186 dull, insensitive, stupid
187 EKSeKYOUseeOWN
188 undertaking★
189 although
190 puts on = assumes, adopts
191 tardy form = slow/sluggish appearance/style★
192 roughness, uncouthness★
193 mind, thought★
194 relish, desire★
195 so it is = thus it does
196 state of the world/worldly affairs
197 worked, shaped (i.e., like "metal")
198 that to which
199 stay ("associate")
200 their likes = those who are similar to them

For who so firm that cannot be seduced?
Caesar doth bear me hard,[201] but he loves Brutus.   310
If I were Brutus now, and he were Cassius,
He should[202] not humor[203] me. I will this night,
In several hands,[204] in at his windows throw,
As if they came from several plebeians,[205]
Writings all tending to the great opinion   315
That Rome holds of his name, wherein obscurely[206]
Caesar's ambition shall be glancèd at.
And after this let Caesar seat him sure,[207]
For we will shake him, or worse days endure.

EXIT

201 bear me hard = cherish/retain a grudge against me★
202 would
203 coax, beguile, influence
204 several hands = different/separate★ handwritings
205 ordinary citizens, commoners
206 indistinctly, inconspicuously
207 seat him sure = make sure he sits safely/securely on his throne/horse

SCENE 3 [Annotations in Study Guide Packet]

A street, that night

THUNDER AND LIGHTNING

ENTER FROM OPPOSITE SIDES CASCA, WITH HIS SWORD
DRAWN, AND CICERO

Cicero   Good even,[1] Casca. Brought[2] you Caesar home?
Why are you breathless, and why stare you so?

Casca   Are not you moved, when all the sway[3] of earth
Shakes like a thing unfirm? O Cicero,
5   I have seen tempests when the scolding[4] winds
Have rived[5] the knotty[6] oaks, and I have seen
Th'ambitious[7] ocean swell and rage and foam,
To be exalted[8] with the threatening[9] clouds.
But never till tonight, never till now,
10   Did I go through a tempest[10] dropping fire.
Either there is a civil strife in heaven,
Or else the world, too saucy with the gods,
Incenses them to send destruction.

Cicero   Why, saw you any thing more wonderful?[11]
15   *Casca*   A common slave – you know him well by sight –

1 evening
2 conducted, escorted
3 rule, governance★
4 brawling, quarrelsome
5 torn apart, split★ (rhymes with "hived, wived," etc.)
6 rugged, gnarled ("old and large")
7 (1) eager, (2) rising, towering
8 to be exalted = in order to be lifted/elevated
9 sternly displeased
10 storm that was
11 astonishing than what I saw

[Handwritten annotations:]
Casca's breathless (from trying to trick Brutus

A tempest dropping fire = lightning
2 reasons for the storm:
1. the gods are fighting
2. the people are being punished by the gods

26

Casca describes 4 omens
— Warnings? omens
— possibly warning
about Ceasar being
King / his interference

Held up his left hand, which did <u>flame and burn</u>
Like twenty torches joined, and yet <u>his hand,</u>
Not sensible of[12] fire, <u>remained unscorched.</u>
Besides — I ha' not since put up[13] my sword —
Against[14] the Capitol I met a lion,   20
Who glazed[15] upon me, and <u>went surly by,</u>
Without annoying[16] me. And there were drawn
<u>Upon[17] a heap a hundred ghastly[18] women,</u>
Transformèd with their fear, <u>who swore they saw</u>
<u>Men all in fire walk up and down the streets.</u>   25
And yesterday <u>the bird of night[19] did sit</u>
Even at noonday upon the marketplace,
Hooting and shrieking. When these prodigies[20]
Do so conjointly[21] meet, let not men say
"These[22] are their reasons, they are natural."   30
For I believe they are portentous[23] things
Unto the climate[24] that they point upon.
Cicero Indeed, it is a strange-disposèd[25] time.
But men may construe things after their fashion,

12 sensible of = feeling
13 put up = put away, re-sheathed
14 opposite, in front of
15 stared
16 harming, injuring★
17 drawn upon = gathered in
18 pale, frightened
19 bird of night = owl
20 (1) marvels, wonders, (2) omens★
21 joined, together
22 i.e., this or this or that are the reasons for such things
23 warning, ominous★
24 place, location, region
25 strange-disposèd = unusually/singularly ordered/inclined

35   Clean[26] from the purpose[27] of the things themselves.

     Comes Caesar to the Capitol tomorrow?

Casca   He doth, for he did bid Antonio

     Send word to you he would be there tomorrow.

Cicero   Good night then, Casca. This disturbèd sky[28]

40   Is not to walk in.[29]

Casca   Farewell, Cicero.

EXIT CICERO

ENTER CASSIUS

Cassius   Who's there?

Casca   A Roman.

Cassius   Casca, by your voice.

Casca   Your ear is good. Cassius, what night[30] is this!

Cassius   A very pleasing night to honest men.

45 *Casca*   Who ever knew the heavens menace so?

Cassius   Those that have known the earth so full of faults.

     For my part, I have walked about the streets,

     Submitting me[31] unto the perilous night,

     And thus unbraced,[32] Casca, as you see,

50   Have bared my bosom to the thunder-stone.[33]

     And when the cross[34] blue lightning seemed to open

26 entirely away
27 meaning, sense
28 upper air, heavens
29 inside ("under")
30 what night = what a night
31 surrendering/exposing myself
32 clothing loosened/unfastened★
33 thunder-stone = thunderbolt
34 (1) crossing, slanting, (2) hostile

The breast of heaven, I did present myself
Even in the aim and very flash of it.

Casca   But wherefore did you so much tempt the heavens?
It is the part of men to fear and tremble,   55
When the most mighty gods by tokens[35] send
Such dreadful heralds[36] to astonish us.

Cassius You are dull,[37] Casca, and those sparks of life
That should be in a Roman you do want,[38]
Or else you use not. You look pale and gaze   60
And put on[39] fear and cast[40] yourself in wonder,
To see the strange impatience[41] of the heavens.
But if you would consider the true cause
Why all these fires, why all these gliding ghosts,
Why birds and beasts, from[42] quality and kind,[43]   65
Why old men, fools, and children calculate,[44]
Why all these things change from their ordinance[45]
Their natures and preformèd faculties
To monstrous[46] quality – why, you shall find
That heaven hath infused them[47] with these spirits,   70
To make them instruments of fear and warning

35 signs, events, portents, omens
36 messengers
37 thick-skulled, stupid
38 lack
39 put on = (1) assume, dress yourself, pretend to, (2) impose (on yourself)
40 send/throw, condemn
41 annoyance, irritation
42 out of, away ("departing from")
43 quality and kind = nature/character/rank and birth/descent★
44 are able to count up (the number of wonders/marvels)
45 usual/ordained arrangement/conditions
46 (1) unnatural, (2) malformed, gigantic★
47 i.e., "all these things"

Unto some monstrous state.[48]
Now could I, Casca, name to thee a man
Most like this dreadful night,
75 That thunders, lightens, opens graves, and roars
As doth the lion in the Capitol,
A man no mightier than thyself or me
In personal action,[49] yet prodigious grown
And fearful,[50] as these strange eruptions[51] are.
80 *Casca* 'Tis Caesar that you mean. Is it not, Cassius?
Cassius Let it be who it is. For Romans now
Have thews[52] and limbs like to their ancestors.
But woe the while,[53] our fathers' minds are dead,
And we are governed with our mothers' spirits,
85 Our yoke and sufferance[54] show us womanish.
Casca Indeed, they say the senators tomorrow
Mean to establish Caesar as a king.
And he shall wear his crown by sea and land,
In every place save here in Italy.
90 *Cassius* I know where I will wear this dagger[55] then.
Cassius from bondage will deliver Cassius.
Therein, ye gods, you make the weak most strong.
Therein, ye gods, you tyrants do defeat.[56]

48 state of affairs
49 actions, deeds
50 terrible, deadful, awful
51 things that burst forth
52 strengths
53 time
54 patient endurance, long suffering
55 i.e., in himself (wear = carry); also, wear = use/show – but subsequent lines
   indicate a suicidal declaration
56 you tyrants do defeat = you defeat tyrants

Nor stony tower, nor walls of beaten brass,
Nor airless dungeon, nor strong links of iron,   95
Can be retentive[57] to the strength of spirit.
But life being weary of these worldly bars,
Never lacks power to dismiss itself.
If I know this, know all the world besides,
That part of tyranny that I do bear   100
I can shake off at pleasure.

THUNDER

Casca   So can I.
    So every bondman[58] in his own hand bears
    The power to cancel his captivity.
Cassius And why should Caesar be a tyrant then?
    Poor man, I know he would not[59] be a wolf,   105
    But[60] that he sees the Romans are but sheep.
    He were[61] no lion, were not Romans hinds.[62]
    Those that with haste will make a mighty fire
    Begin it with weak[63] straws. What trash is Rome,
    What rubbish and what offal,[64] when it serves   110
    For the base matter to[65] illuminate
    So vile[66] a thing as Caesar! But O grief,

---

57 hold, keep back, confine
58 serf, slave★
59 would not = does not wish
60 except
61 would be (subjunctive)
62 domestic servants, farm laborers
63 flexible, pliable
64 dross, refuse, waste ("garbage")
65 used to
66 disgusting, despicable★

Where hast thou led me? I (perhaps) speak this
Before a willing bondman. Then I know
115   My answer[67] must be made. But I am armed,
And dangers are to me indifferent.[68]

    Casca   You speak to Casca, and to such a man
That[69] is no fleering[70] telltale. Hold,[71] my hand.[72]
Be factious[73] for redress of all these griefs,
120   And I will set this foot of mine as far
As who[74] goes farthest.

    Cassius   *(shaking hands)* There's a bargain made.
Now know you, Casca, I have moved already
Some certain of the noblest-minded Romans
To undergo[75] with me an enterprise
125   Of honorable-dangerous consequence.
And I do know by this[76] they stay[77] for me
In Pompey's porch.[78] For now,[79] this fearful night,
There is no stir or walking in the streets,
And the complexion of the element
130   In[80] favor's[81] like the work we have in hand,

67 response (physical?)
68 inDIfeRENT
69 such a man that = a man who
70 grinning, obsequious
71 stop, enough
72 my hand = here is my hand
73 seditious
74 whoever
75 bear, sustain, partake of
76 now
77 wait★
78 portico/covered walkway (built by Pompey, beside his open-air theater)
79 the time being
80 Folio: is; all editors emend
81 favor's = favor is = disposition/inclination is

Most bloody, fiery, and most terrible.

Casca   Stand close[82] awhile, for here comes one in haste.

Cassius   'Tis Cinna,[83] I do know him by his gait,[84]

He is a friend.

ENTER CINNA

              Cinna, where haste you so?

Cinna   To find out you. Who's that? Metellus Cimber?[85]   135

Cassius   No, it is Casca, one incorporate[86]

   To our attempts. Am I not stayed for, Cinna?

Cinna   I am glad on't. What a fearful night is this!

   There's two or three of us have seen strange sights.

Cassius   Am I not stayed for? Tell me.

Cinna   Yes, you are.   140

   O Cassius, if you could

   But win the noble Brutus to our party –

Cassius   Be you content.[87] Good Cinna, take this paper,

   And look you lay it in the praetor's[88] chair,

   Where Brutus may but[89] find it. And throw this[90]   145

   In at his window; set this up[91] with wax

   Upon old Brutus' statue. All this done,

   Repair[92] to Pompey's porch, where you shall find us.

82 to the side, in concealment
83 SIna
84 walk, carriage, bearing
85 meTELlus SIMber
86 one incorporate = someone/a person united/associated
87 calm, not uneasy, satisfied★
88 Brutus: an administrative judgeship★ (to which Caesar had appointed him)
89 Brutus may but = only Brutus may
90 (emphasized)
91 set this up = affix this (emphasized)
92 go, make your way

Is Decius[93] Brutus and Trebonius[94] there?

150   *Cinna*   All but Metellus Cimber, and he's gone
        To seek you at your house. Well, I will hie,[95]
        And so bestow[96] these papers as you bade me.
    Cassius   That done, repair to Pompey's theater.[97]

EXIT CINNA

        Come Casca, you and I will yet ere day
155   See Brutus at his house. Three parts of him
        Is ours already, and the man entire
        Upon the next encounter yields him ours.[98]

    Casca   O, he sits high in all the people's hearts.
        And that which would appear offense[99] in us,
160   His countenance,[100] like richest[101] alchemy,
        Will change to virtue and to worthiness.

    Cassius   Him and his worth and our great need of him
        You have right well conceited.[102] Let us go,
        For it is after midnight, and ere day
165   We will awake him and be sure of him.

EXEUNT

---

93 DEEshus
94 triBONyus
95 hurry★
96 place, put, deposit★
97 see n.78, above
98 yields him ours = will give him to us/render him ours
99 (1) injurious, harmful, (2) unpleasant, offensive, disgraceful★
100 support, show of goodwill, patronage
101 the strongest/most powerful
102 conceived, grasped, thought★

Act 2

Rome, Brutus' garden

ENTER BRUTUS

Brutus What, Lucius, ho!
  I cannot, by the progress of the stars,
  Give[1] guess how near to day.[2] Lucius, I say!
  I would[3] it were my fault to sleep so soundly.[4]
  When, Lucius, when? Awake, I say! What, Lucius!   5

ENTER LUCIUS

Lucius Called you,[5] my lord?
Brutus Get me[6] a taper[7] in my study, Lucius.
  When it is lighted, come and call me here.

1 make a
2 near to day = near to daylight / dawn it is
3 wish
4 so soundly = as soundly as you do, Lucius
5 called you = did you call
6 get me = put ("fetch for me")
7 candle

Lucius I will, my lord.

EXIT LUCIUS

10   *Brutus* It must be by his[8] death. And for my part,
        I know no personal cause[9] to spurn at[10] him,
        But for[11] the general. He would be crowned.
        How that might change his nature, there's the question.
        It is the bright day that brings forth the adder,
        And that craves[12] wary walking. Crown[13] him that,[14]
        And then I grant[15] we put a sting in him,
        That at his will he may do danger with.
        The abuse[16] of greatness is when it disjoins[17]
        Remorse[18] from power. And to speak truth of Caesar,
20   I have not known when his affections swayed
        More than his reason.[19] But 'tis a common proof[20]
        That lowliness[21] is young ambition's ladder,
        Whereto[22] the climber upward turns his face.
        But when he once attains the upmost round[23]
25   He then unto the ladder turns his back,

        8 Caesar's
        9 personal cause = individual/private grounds/reason★
        10 spurn at = oppose, kick at★
        11 but for = except/only for
        12 demands, requires
        13 adorn, invest
        14 with that (i.e., the power of a king/emperor)
        15 agree, admit, promise
        16 misuse, perversion, corruption★
        17 separates, severs
        18 compassion, pity
        19 rationality, intellect, sense★
        20 fact, truth, experience
        21 humility, humbleness★
        22 to/toward which
        23 rung

Its commonly known that humility is always there until you cant go anywhere.

Looks in the clouds, scorning the base degrees[24]

humility →

ladder of power

By which he did ascend. So Caesar may.

Then lest he may, prevent.[25] And, since the quarrel[26]

Will bear no color for[27] the thing he is,

Fashion[28] it thus: that what he is, augmented,

Caesar may turn his back on humility [30]

Would run to these and these extremities,

And therefore think him as[29] a serpent's egg

Which hatched would, as his kind,[30] grow mischievous,[31]

And kill him in the shell. *he must stop it before it happens*

ENTER LUCIUS

Lucius The taper burneth in your closet,[32] sir.   35

Searching the window for a flint,[33] I found

This paper, thus sealed up, and I am sure

a letter   } *delivered by Lucius*

It did not lie there when I went to bed.

LUCIUS GIVES HIM THE LETTER

Brutus Get you to bed again, it is not day.

Is not tomorrow,[34] boy,[35] the Ides[36] of March?   40

March 15; Caesar should be weary

24 steps, stages

25 prevent/stop★ it/him

26 cause for complaint

27 color for = show of reason/pretext/excuse because of

28 (verb) shape, form, frame★

29 like

30 as his kind = like his descent/natural disposition

31 harmful, disastrous★

32 private room, inner chamber★

33 i.e., a stone that, struck with metal, gives off sparks that enable the lighting of a fire

34 i.e., night is a continuation of day, and the morning, marking the start of a new day, had not yet come

35 servant★

36 Folio: first; most editors emend

Lucius I know not, sir.

Brutus Look in the calendar, and bring me word.

Lucius I will, sir.

EXIT LUCIUS

Brutus The exhalations whizzing[37] in the air

45   Give so much light that I may read by them.

HE OPENS THE LETTER AND READS

"Brutus, thou sleep'st. Awake, and see thyself.
Shall Rome, etcetera. Speak, strike, redress!"[38]
Brutus, thou sleep'st: awake!"

Such instigations[39] have been often dropped
50   Where I have took[40] them up.

"Shall Rome, etcetera." Thus must I piece it out:[41]
Shall Rome stand[42] under one man's awe? What, Rome?
My ancestors did from the streets of Rome
The Tarquin drive, when he was called a king.[43]
55   "Speak, strike, redress!" Am I entreated
To speak and strike? O Rome, I make thee promise:[44]
If the redress will follow, thou receivest[45]
Thy full petition[46] at the hand of Brutus!

37 exhalations whizzing = meteors hissing/sizzling/rushing
38 restore, reestablish
39 goading, incitements
40 took = taken = picked
41 piece it out = complete/extend it
42 remain, stay
43 see act 1, scene 2, n.111
44 make thee promise = declare to/assure you
45 will receive
46 prayer, request

38

ENTER LUCIUS

Lucius Sir, March is wasted[47] fifteen days. — *Its the ides today*
of march

KNOCKING WITHIN

Brutus 'Tis good. Go to the gate, somebody knocks.   60

EXIT LUCIUS

Since Cassius first did whet[48] me against Caesar,
I have not slept.   *urge*
Between the acting of a dreadful[49] thing
And the first motion,[50] all the interim is
Like a phantasma, or a hideous dream. — *a nightmare*   65
The genius[51] and the mortal instruments
Are then in council, and the state of man,
Like to a little kingdom, suffers[52] then
The nature[53] of an insurrection.

ENTER LUCIUS

Lucius Sir, 'tis your brother[54] Cassius at the door,   70
     Who doth desire to see you.
Brutus   Is he alone?
Lucius No, sir, there are moe[55] with him.
                              more

47 diminished/lessened by
48 incite, urge
49 awe-inspiring
50 first motion = original excitement/mental agitation/prompting/impulse
51 guiding spirit
52 undergoes, endures, experiences
53 necessary/innate characteristics
54 Cassius was married to Brutus' sister; by the usages of Shakespeare's time he
   is therefore Brutus' brother, not brother-in-law
55 more

Brutus   Do you know[56] them?

Lucius No, sir, their hats are plucked[57] about their ears,
    And half their faces buried in their cloaks,
75 That by no means I may discover them
    By any mark[58] of favor.

Brutus   ~~Sign~~   Let 'em enter.

EXIT LUCIUS

    They are the faction.[59] O conspiracy,
    Sham'st thou to show thy dangerous brow by night,
    When evils are most free?[60] O, then by day
80 Where wilt thou find a cavern dark enough
    To mask thy monstrous visage? Seek none, conspiracy.
    Hide it in smiles and affability.
    For if thou path thy native semblance on,[61]
    Not Erebus[62] itself were dim enough
85 To hide thee from prevention.

ENTER CASSIUS, CASCA, DECIUS BRUTUS, CINNA,
METELLUS CIMBER, AND TREBONIUS

Cassius I think we are too bold[63] upon your rest.
    Good morrow,[64] Brutus, do we trouble you?

Brutus I have been up this hour, awake all night.

56 recognize
57 pulled
58 sign, indication
59 dissenting/rebellious group
60 unrestrained, unrestricted, at liberty
61 path thy native semblance on = go along with your natural appearance
62 the dark places between the earth and Hades/Hell (ERiBUS)
63 presumptuous, forward, audacious, daring
64 morning

Know I these men that come along with you?

Cassius　　　Yes, every man of them, and no man here　　　　90
　　　But honors you. And every one doth wish
　　　You had but that opinion of yourself
　　　Which every noble Roman bears of you.
　　　This is Trebonius.

Brutus　　　　　　He is welcome hither.

Cassius　　　This, Decius Brutus.

Brutus　　　　　　　　He is welcome too.　　　　95

Cassius　　　This, Casca; this, Cinna; and this, Metellus Cimber.

Brutus　　　They are all welcome.

　　What watchful[65] cares do interpose themselves

　　Betwixt your eyes and night?

Cassius　　　　　　Shall I entreat a word?

BRUTUS AND CASSIUS WHISPER

Decius Brutus　Here lies the east. Doth not the day break here?　100

Casca　　　No.

Cinna　　　O pardon, sir, it doth, and yon gray lines,

　　That fret[66] the clouds, are messengers of day.

Casca　　　You shall confess that you are both deceived.

　　Here, as I point my sword, the sun arises,　　　　105

　　Which is a great way growing[67] on the south,

　　Weighing[68] the youthful season of the year.

　　Some two months hence, up higher toward the north

　　He first presents his fire,[69] and the high east

65 sleepless, wakeful
66 (1) variegate, checker, interlace, (2) adorn
67 increasing ("moving toward")
68 considering
69 he first presents his fire = the sun will come up ("first display its rays")

110   Stands, as[70] the Capitol, directly here.

    Brutus   Give me your hands all over,[71] one by one.

    Cassius And let us swear our resolution.[72]

    Brutus   No, not an oath. If not the face of men,[73]

    The sufferance[74] of our souls, the time's abuse –

115   If these be motives weak, break off betimes,[75]

    And every man hence, to his idle[76] bed.

    So let high-sighted[77] tyranny range[78] on,

    Till each man drop by lottery.[79] But if these

    (As I am sure they do) bear fire[80] enough

120   To kindle cowards and to steel with valor

    The melting spirits of women, then countrymen,

    What need we any spur but our own cause

    To prick[81] us to redress? What other bond

    Than secret[82] Romans, that have spoke the word

125   And will not palter?[83] And what other oath

    Than honesty to honesty engaged[84]

    That this shall be, or we will fall[85] for it?

70 as does, like
71 all over = each of you, one after another
72 (1) decision, agreement, (2) conviction, certainty, (3) determination, resolve
73 the face of men = (?) the faces of our fellow citizens
74 suffering, grief
75 at once, speedily, before it's too late★
76 empty ("out of use")★
77 supercilious
78 (1) proceed, (2) wander
79 drop by lottery = fall/die by casting of lots/chance
80 heat, spirit, ardor, passion
81 urge, drive, provoke
82 close-mouthed
83 shift, alter, shuffle ("equivocate")
84 pledged
85 die

Swear priests and cowards and men cautelous,[86]
Old feeble carrions,[87] and such suffering[88] souls
That welcome wrongs. Unto bad causes swear   130
Such creatures as men doubt,[89] but do not stain
The even[90] virtue of our enterprise,
Nor the insuppressive[91] mettle of our spirits,
To think that or[92] our cause or our performance
Did need an oath, when every drop of blood   135
That every Roman bears, and nobly bears,
Is guilty of a several bastardy[93]
If he do break the smallest particle
Of any promise that hath passed[94] from him.

Cassius   But what of Cicero? Shall we sound[95] him?   140
  I think he will stand very strong[96] with us.

Casca   Let us not leave him out.

Cinna   No, by no means.

Metellus Cimber O let us have him, for his silver hairs
  Will purchase us a good opinion
  And buy men's voices to commend our deeds.   145
  It shall be said his judgment ruled our hands,
  Our youths and wildness[97] shall no whit appear,

86 deceitful, wily, crafty
87 carcasses, corpses
88 patient, submissive
89 (1) mistrust, suspect, (2) fear, dread
90 uniform, straightforward, level★
91 insuppressible
92 either
93 several bastardy = distinct proof of not being a true Roman
94 come
95 (1) test, investigate, (2) approach
96 strongly, forcefully, solidly
97 fierceness, incivility

But all be buried in his gravity.[98]

Brutus O name him not. Let us not break[99] with him;

150 For he will never follow anything
That other men begin.

Cassius Then leave him out.

Casca Indeed, he is not fit.[100]

Decius Brutus Shall no man else be touched but only Caesar?

Cassius Decius, well urged.[101] I think it is not meet[102]

155 Mark Antony, so well beloved of Caesar,
Should outlive Caesar. We shall find of him[103]
A shrewd contriver.[104] And you know his means,[105]
If he improve them,[106] may well stretch so far
As to annoy us all. Which to prevent,

160 Let Antony and Caesar fall together.

Brutus Our course will seem too bloody, Caius Cassius,
To cut the head off and then hack the limbs,
Like wrath in death and envy afterwards.
For Antony is but a limb of Caesar,

165 Let us be sacrificers, but not butchers, Caius.
We all stand up against the spirit of Caesar,
And in the spirit of men there is no blood.
O that we then could come by[107] Caesar's spirit

98 influence, authority, seriousness
99 violate the secrecy of our agreement/pledge, reveal ourselves
100 appropriate, suitable
101 brought forward, introduced, pressed★
102 meet that
103 of him = him to be
104 schemer, plotter
105 resources, wealth★
106 improve them = use them well, make use of them
107 come by = reach ("come near")

And not dismember Caesar! But (alas)
Caesar must bleed for it. And gentle friends,   170
Let's kill him boldly, but not wrathfully.
Let's carve him as a dish fit for the gods,
Not hew[108] him as a carcass fit for hounds.
And let our hearts, as subtle[109] masters do,
Stir up their servants to an act of rage   175
And after seem to chide 'em. This shall make
Our purpose necessary and not envious.
Which so appearing to the common eyes,
We shall be called purgers, not murderers.
And for Mark Antony, think not of him.   180
For he can do no more than Caesar's arm
When Caesar's head is off.

Cassius   Yet I fear him,
For in the engrafted[110] love he bears to Caesar –

Brutus   Alas, good Cassius, do not think of him.
If he love Caesar, all that he can do   185
Is to himself, take thought and die for Caesar,
And that were much[111] he should.[112] For he is given
To sports, to wildness and much company.
Trebonius There is no fear in him. Let him not die,
For he will live, and laugh at this hereafter.   190

CLOCK STRIKES

Brutus   Peace, count the clock.

108 chop, hack
109 fine, dexterous, skillful, clever
110 firmly set
111 to a high degree what
112 ought to do

45

Cassius   The clock hath stricken three.

Trebonius   'Tis time to part.

Cassius   But it is doubtful yet

    Whether Caesar will come forth today or no.

    For he is superstitious grown of late,

195   Quite[113] from the main[114] opinion he held once

    Of fantasy,[115] of dreams and ceremonies.

    It may be these apparent[116] prodigies, *omens*

    The unaccustomed terror of this night,

    And the persuasion of his augurers,[117]

200   May hold him from the Capitol today.

Caesar is weary; the augurers are warning him against going there some—

Decius Brutus Never fear that. If he be so resolved,[118]

    I can o'ersway[119] him. For he loves to hear

    That unicorns may be betrayed with trees,[120]

    And bears with glasses, elephants with holes,[121]

205   Lions with toils,[122] and men with flatterers.

    But when I tell him he hates flatterers,

    He says he does, being then most flattered.

    Let me work.[123]

'Tis the ides of March

113 strongly away/different
114 vigorous, strong
115 visions, imagined things ("imagination")★
116 visible, plainly seen, conspicuous
117 diviners, readers and interpreters of omens/signs
118 (1) decided, determined, convinced, (2) informed, satisfied, assured★
119 persuade, lead, overpower
120 betrayed with trees = deceived/seduced into running his horn into a tree
    trunk and thus trapping himself
121 bears: by deceiving mirrors; elephants: by disguised/covered-over holes in
    the ground
122 traps, snares ("nets")
123 do the business, perform, make it happen

	For I can give his humor[124] the true bent,[125]	
	And I will bring him to the Capitol.	210
Cassius	Nay, we will all of us be there to fetch him.	
Brutus	By the eighth hour, is that the uttermost?[126]	
Cinna	Be that the uttermost, and fail not then.	
Metellus Cimber	Caius Ligarius doth bear Caesar hard,[127]	
	Who rated[128] him for speaking well of Pompey:	215
	I wonder none of you have thought of him.	
Brutus	Now, good Metellus, go along by him.[129]	
	He loves me well, and I have given him reasons.[130]	
	Send him but[131] hither, and I'll fashion him.	
Cassius	The morning comes upon 's. We'll leave you,	220
	Brutus.	
	And friends, disperse yourselves, but all remember	
	What you have said, and show yourselves true Romans.	
Brutus	Good gentlemen, look fresh and merrily.[132]	
	Let not our looks put on[133] our purposes,	
	But bear[134] it as our Roman actors do,	225
	With untired spirits and formal constancy.[135]	
	And so good morrow to you every one.	

124 mood, disposition★
125 true bent = reliable/secure/steady turn/inclination
126 latest
127 CEYEyus liGARyus DOTH bear CAEsar HARD
128 scolded/reproved vehemently/angrily
129 go along by him = visit him, go to his house
130 grounds, cause
131 send him but = just send him
132 fresh and merrily = bright/vigorous/easy and cheerful
133 put on = draw attention to
134 (1) maintain, support, sustain, (2) impersonate
135 formal constancy = apparent/external steadiness/firmness/fortitude★

EXEUNT ALL BUT BRUTUS

Boy! Lucius! Fast asleep? It is no matter,
Enjoy the honey-heavy dew[136] of slumber.
230 Thou hast no figures,[137] nor no fantasies,
Which busy care draws in the brains of men.
Therefore thou sleep'st so sound.

ENTER PORTIA

Portia   Brutus, my lord.
Brutus Portia, what mean you? Wherefore rise you now?
It is not for[138] your health thus to commit[139]
235 Your weak condition to the raw cold morning.
Portia Nor for yours neither. Y'have ungently,[140] Brutus,
Stole from my bed. And yesternight at supper
You suddenly arose, and walked about,
Musing and sighing, with your arms a-cross.[141]
240 And when I asked you what the matter was,
You stared upon me with ungentle looks.
I urged you further, then you scratched your head,
And too impatiently[142] stamp'd with your foot.[143]
Yet[144] I insisted, yet you answered not,
245 But with an angry wafture[145] of your hand

136 honey-heavy dew = sweetly heavy refreshment
137 mental images
138 good/favorable for
139 entrust
140 discourteously
141 crossed
142 irritably, irascibly
143 andTOO imPAtientLY stamp'd WITH your FOOT
144 still
145 wave

Gave sign for me to leave you. So I did,
Fearing to strengthen that impatience[146]
Which seemed too much enkindled, and withal[147]
Hoping it was but an effect of humor,
Which sometime hath his hour with every man.   250
It will not let you eat, nor talk, nor sleep,
And could it work so much upon your shape
As it hath much prevailed on your condition,
I should not know you, Brutus. Dear my lord,
Make me acquainted with your cause of grief.   255

Brutus I am not well in health, and that is all.

Portia Brutus is wise, and were he not in health
   He would embrace[148] the means to come by it.[149]

Brutus Why so I do. Good Portia, go to bed.

Portia Is Brutus sick? And is it physical   260
   To walk unbraced and suck up[150] the humors[151]
   Of the dank[152] morning? What, is Brutus sick?
   And will he steal out of his wholesome bed
   To dare the vile contagion of the night
   And tempt the rheumy[153] and unpurgèd[154] air   265
   To add unto his sickness? No, my Brutus,
   You have some sick offense within your mind,

146 imPAseeANCE
147 moreover, in addition, nevertheless★
148 avail himself of
149 health
150 suck up = breathe in
151 vapors, exhalation, moisture
152 damp
153 damp, rheumatic
154 not cleansed

Which by the right and virtue[155] of my place[156]
I ought to know of. And upon my knees,
270   I charm[157] you, by my once-commended beauty,
By all your vows of love and that <u>great vow</u>
marriage
<u>Which did incorporate and make us one,</u>
That you unfold[158] to me – your self, your half –
Why you are heavy.[159] And what men tonight
275   Have had resort[160] to you. For here have been
Some six or seven, who did hide their faces
Even from darkness.

Brutus   Kneel not, gentle Portia.

Portia   I should not need, if you were gentle Brutus.
Within the bond of marriage, tell me, Brutus,
280   Is it excepted[161] I should know no secrets
That appertain[162] to you? Am I yourself
But[163] (as it were) in sort[164] or limitation,
To keep[165] with you at meals, comfort[166] your bed,
And talk to you sometimes? Dwell I but in the suburbs
285   Of your good pleasure? If it be no more,
Portia is Brutus' harlot,[167] not his wife.

          basically, if im your wife, you talk to me,
              otherwise I'm just your whore!

155 power
156 position
157 conjure, entreat
158 reveal, disclose
159 burdened, gloomy
160 access
161 an exception to our oneness that
162 belong, are appropriate/proper
163 only
164 a certain/different kind
165 stay, keep company
166 (1) gladden, cheer, entertain, (2) invigorate, refresh, relieve★
167 whore, prostitute

Brutus You are my true and honorable[168] wife, *Don't call yourself that!*

As dear[169] to me as are the ruddy[170] drops

That visit[171] my sad[172] heart. *If it's true, tell me what's up*

Portia If this were true, then should I know this secret. 290

I grant I am a woman, but withal *I know I am a girl, but still*

A woman that Lord Brutus took to wife.

I grant I am a woman, but withal

A woman well-reputed, Cato's[173] daughter.

Think you I am no stronger than my sex, *mark of feminism* 295

Being so fathered and so husbanded?

Tell me your counsels,[174] *troubles* I will not disclose 'em.

I have made strong proof[175] of my constancy,

Giving myself a voluntary wound

Here, in the thigh. Can I bear that with patience, 300

And not my husband's secrets?

Brutus   O ye gods, *I don't deserve my wife*

Render me[176] worthy of this noble wife!

KNOCKING WITHIN

Hark, hark, one[177] knocks. Portia, go in a while,

And by and by[178] thy bosom shall partake[179]

168 ONorABle
169 worthy, precious★
170 red
171 come to
172 (1) heavy, somber, mournful, (2) orderly, regular
173 Cato was celebrated for his totally moral character; a fierce opponent of
    Julius Caesar, he committed suicide after Caesar had triumphed
174 (1) deliberations, conversations, (2) plans, purposes
175 (1) demonstration, (2) test, trial
176 render me = cause/make me
177 someone
178 soon, shortly
179 share, be informed of

305   The secrets of my heart.
      All my engagements[180] I will construe to thee,
      All the charactery[181] of my sad brows.
      Leave me with haste.

EXIT PORTIA

Lucius, who's[182] that knocks?

ENTER LUCIUS WITH LIGARIUS

Lucius   He is a sick man that would speak with you.
310 *Brutus*   Caius Ligarius, that Metellus spake of.
      Boy, stand aside. Caius Ligarius, how?[183]
      Ligarius   Vouchsafe[184] good morrow from a feeble tongue.
      Brutus   O what a time have you chose out,[185] brave Caius,
      To wear a kerchief.[186] Would you were not sick.
315 *Ligarius*   I am not sick, if Brutus have in hand
      Any exploit worthy the name of honor.

If you are doing something worthy of honor, I am not sick

      Brutus   Such an exploit have I in hand, Ligarius,
      Had you a healthful[187] ear to hear of it.
      Ligarius   By all the gods that Romans bow before,
320   I here discard my sickness! (*removes kerchief*) Soul of Rome,
      Brave son, derived from honorable loins,
      Thou like an exorcist[188] hast conjured up

---

180 agreements, undertakings, promises, obligations
181 meaning (i.e., that which is expressed by such visible signs/symbolic
      representations)
182 who is it
183 how are you
184 let me bestow/confer/grant*
185 chose out = picked out, selected
186 wear a kerchief = be sick (kerchief = head covering for the sick)
187 healthy
188 person who drives out evil spirits

My mortified[189] spirit. Now bid me run,

And I will strive[190] with things impossible,

Yea, get the better of them. What's to do?   325

Brutus   A piece of work that will make sick men whole.

Ligarius But are not some whole that we must make sick?

Brutus   That must we also. What it is, my Caius,

I shall unfold to thee as we are going

To whom[191] it must be done.

Ligarius   Set on your foot,   330

And with a heart new-fired[192] I follow you,

To do I know not what. But it sufficeth

That Brutus leads me on.

Brutus   Follow me, then.

EXEUNT

189 numbed, insensible
190 fight
191 Caesar
192 newly kindled/lighted

53

SCENE 2

Caesar's house

THUNDER AND LIGHTNING

ENTER CAESAR, IN HIS NIGHTGOWN[1]

Caesar   Nor heaven nor earth have been at peace tonight.

Thrice hath Calphurnia in her sleep cried out,

"Help, ho, they murder Caesar!" Who's within?[2]

Calphurnia is dreaming of Caesar being murdered

ENTER SERVANT

Servant   My lord?

5   *Caesar*   Go bid the priests do present[3] sacrifice

And bring me their opinions of success.

Servant   I will, my lord.

EXIT SERVANT

ENTER CALPHURNIA

Calphurnia What mean you, Caesar? Think you to walk forth?

You shall[4] not stir out of your house today. You're not leaving the house today

10 *Caesar*   Caesar shall forth. The things that threatened me

Ne'er looked but on my back. When they shall see

The face of Caesar, they are vanishèd.

Calphurnia Caesar, I never stood on[5] ceremonies,

Yet now they fright me. There is one within,[6]

I never worried about omens, but now I'm scared

1 dressing gown? nightgown? (in act 4, scene 3, gown = dressing gown)
2 i.e., what servant is there to attend on me?
3 immediate, without delay
4 must, should
5 stood on = was scrupulous/meticulously careful about, valued
6 one within = someone inside

Besides[7] the things that we have heard and seen   15
Recounts most horrid sights seen by the watch.[8]
A lioness hath whelpèd[9] in the streets,
And graves have yawned,[10] and yielded up their dead.
Fierce fiery warriors fought upon the clouds
In ranks[11] and squadrons and right form[12] of war,   20
Which drizzled blood upon the Capitol.
The noise of battle hurtled[13] in the air,
Horses did neigh, and dying men did groan,
And ghosts did shriek and squeal about the streets.
O Caesar, these things are beyond all use,   25
And I do fear them.

Caesar   What can be avoided
Whose end[14] is purposed by the mighty gods?
Yet Caesar shall go forth. For these predictions
Are to the world in general, as[15] to Caesar.

Calphurnia When beggars die, there are no comets seen.   30
The heavens themselves blaze forth the death of princes.

Caesar   Cowards die many times before their deaths,
The valiant never taste of death but once.
Of all the wonders that I yet have heard,
It seems to me most strange that men should fear,[16]   35

7 who in addition to
8 guards, watchmen, sentinels
9 given birth
10 opened wide
11 military order, lined up abreast and in rows
12 right form = straight/correct/proper arrangement
13 was cast/flung
14 (1) result, completion, (2) aim, goal
15 as well as
16 be afraid

Seeing that death, a necessary end,
Will come when it will come.

ENTER SERVANT

What say the augurers?
Servant   They would not have you to stir forth today.
Plucking the entrails of an offering forth,[17]
40   They could not find a heart within the beast.
Caesar   The gods do this in shame of cowardice.
Metaphor   Caesar should be a beast without a heart
If he should stay at home today for fear.
No, Caesar shall not. Danger knows full well
45   That Caesar is more dangerous than he.   he is stronger / braver
We are two lions littered in one day,   from danger
And I the elder and more terrible,
And Caesar shall go forth.
Calphurnia   You are too confident   Alas, my lord,
Your wisdom is consumed[18] in confidence.
50   Do not go forth today. Call it my fear
That keeps you in the house, and not your own.
We'll send Mark Antony to the Senate house,
And he shall say you are not well today:
(*kneeling*) Let me, upon my knee, prevail in this.
55   *Caesar*   Mark Antony shall say I am not well,
And for thy humor, I will stay at home.

ENTER DECIUS BRUTUS

Here's Decius Brutus, he shall tell them so.

17 plucking . . . forth = pulling out
18 decomposed, wasted away, destroyed

Decius Brutus Caesar, all hail! Good morrow, worthy Caesar.

I come to fetch you to the Senate house.

Caesar   And you are come in very happy[19] time,   60

To bear my greeting to the Senators

And tell them that I will not come today.

Cannot, is false, and that I dare not, falser.

I will not come today. Tell them so, Decius.

Calphurnia Say he is sick.

Caesar   Shall Caesar send a lie?   65

Have I in conquest stretched mine arm so far,[20]

To be[21] afraid to tell graybeards the truth?   *Tell them I refuse to go.*

Decius, go tell them Caesar will not come.

Decius Brutus Most mighty Caesar, let me know some cause,

Lest I be laughed at when I tell them so.   70

Caesar   The cause is in my will. I will not come,

That is enough to satisfy the Senate.   *give me a reason or he will laugh at me*

But for your private satisfaction,[22]

Because I love you, I will let you know.

Calphurnia here, my wife, stays me at home.   75

She dreamt tonight[23] she saw my statue,

Which like a fountain with an hundred spouts[24]

Did run pure blood. And many lusty[25] Romans

Came smiling, and did bathe their hands in it.

And these does she apply for warnings and portents,   80

19 fortunate, favorable
20 so far = so/as far as I have
21 to be = that I am
22 SAtisFACseeOWN
23 last night
24 drainage pipes
25 joyful, merry

And evils imminent; and on her knee
Hath begged that I will stay at home today.
Decius Brutus This dream is all amiss interpreted,
It was a vision fair and fortunate.
85 Your statue spouting blood in many pipes,
In which so many smiling Romans bathed,
Signifies that from you great Rome shall suck
Reviving blood, and that great men shall press
For tinctures,[26] stains,[27] relics[28] and cognizance.[29]
90 This by Calphurnia's dream is signified.
Caesar And this way have you well expounded it.
Decius Brutus I have, when you have heard what I can say.
And know it now. The Senate have concluded
To give this day a crown to mighty Caesar.
95 If you shall send them word you will not come,
Their minds may change. Besides, it were a mock[30]
Apt[31] to be rendered,[32] for someone to say
"Break up[33] the Senate till another time,
When Caesar's wife shall meet with better dreams."
100 If Caesar hide himself, shall they not whisper
"Lo, Caesar is afraid"?
Pardon me, Caesar, for[34] my dear, dear love
To your proceeding[35] bids me tell you this.

26 tastes, flavors
27 bloodstained cloth
28 mementos
29 as tokens
30 derisive/contemptuous remark
31 likely, ready, fit★
32 given, said★
33 break up = dissolve, disband
34 because, since
35 advancement, progress

And reason to my love is liable.[36] *subjuctive*

Caesar How foolish do your fears seem now, Calphurnia.   105

I am ashamèd I did yield to them.

Give me my robe, for I will go.

against Caesar

ENTER PUBLIUS, BRUTUS, LIGARIUS, METELLUS,
CASCA, TREBONIUS, AND CINNA

And look where[37] Publius is come to fetch me.

Publius Good morrow, Caesar.

Caesar   Welcome, Publius.

What Brutus, are you stirred[38] so early too?   110

Good morrow, Casca. Caius Ligarius,

Caesar was ne'er so much your enemy

As that same ague which hath made you lean.

What is't o'clock?

Brutus   Caesar, 'tis strucken eight. *it's 8 o'clock*

Caesar I thank you for your pains and courtesy.   115

ENTER ANTONY

See, Antony, that revels[39] long o' nights,

Is notwithstanding up.[40] Good morrow, Antony.

Antony So[41] to most noble Caesar. *it's the same*

Caesar   Bid them prepare within.[42]

I am to blame to be thus waited for.

36 answerable, subject (i.e., whatever reason may *want* to say, love takes charge)
37 look where = behold, see
38 in motion, moving about, roused
39 makes merry ("goes partying")
40 not withstanding up = up in spite of that
41 the same
42 them = servants; what they prepare is the wine mentioned in line 126, just
  below

120   Now Cinna, now Metellus. What, Trebonius!
       I have an hour's talk in store[43] for you. *I have to talk to you*
       Remember that you call[44] on me today. *for an hour*
       Be near me, that I may remember you.[45] *answer me*
       Trebonius Caesar, I will. (*aside*) And so near will I be
125   That your best friends shall wish I had been further.
       Caesar   Good friends, go in, and taste some wine with me,
       And we, like friends,[46] will straightway go together.
       Brutus   (*aside*) That every like[47] is not the same, O Caesar,
       The heart of Brutus yearns to think upon.

EXEUNT

---

43 in store = waiting, reserved
44 are scheduled to call
45 you are coming, later today
46 like friends = as friends do
47 semblance, appearance

SCENE 3

A street near the Capitol

ENTER ARTEMIDORUS,[1] READING A PAPER[2]

[handwritten: listen to this Caesar]

Artemidorus "Caesar, beware of Brutus, take heed of Cassius,
come not near Casca, have an eye to Cinna, trust not
Trebonius, mark well Metellus Cimber, Decius Brutus loves
thee not, thou hast wronged Caius Ligarius. There is but one
mind in all these men, and it is bent against Caesar. If thou   5
beest not immortal, look about you. Security[3] gives way to
conspiracy. The mighty gods defend[4] thee!

"Thy lover,[5] *[handwritten: your friend]* "

"ARTEMIDORUS."

Here will I stand till Caesar pass along,   10
And as[6] a suitor[7] will I give him this.
My heart laments that virtue cannot live
Out of[8] the teeth[9] of emulation.[10]
If thou read this, O Caesar, thou mayest live.[11]
If not, the Fates with traitors do contrive.[12]   15

[handwritten: The Fates will let traitors plot]

EXIT

1 AR-te-mi-DOR-us, a Greek scholar friendly with those in Brutus' circle
2 document
3 safety
4 protect★
5 friend★
6 like
7 petitioner
8 out of = away/distant from
9 i.e., that with which envy bites
10 ambition, envy
11 perhaps a rhyme convention, perhaps an actual rhyme, "live" pronounced,
   here, like "strive, hive"
12 scheme, plot

SCENE 4

Along the same street, in front of Brutus' house

ENTER PORTIA AND LUCIUS

Portia I prithee,[1] boy, run to the Senate house.
Stay not to answer me, but get thee gone.
Why dost thou stay?
Lucius   To know my errand, madam.
Portia I would have had thee there, and here again,
5   Ere I can tell thee what thou shouldst do there.
O constancy, be strong upon my side,
Set a huge mountain 'tween my heart and tongue.
I have a man's mind, but a[2] woman's might.
How hard it is for women to keep counsel!
Art thou here yet?
10 *Lucius*   Madam, what should I do?
Run to the Capitol, and nothing else?
And so return to you, and nothing else?
Portia Yes, bring me word, boy, if thy lord look well,
For he went sickly forth. And take good note
15   What Caesar doth, what suitors press to him.
Hark boy! What noise is that?
Lucius   I hear none, madam.
Portia Prithee, listen well.
I heard a bustling rumor,[3] like a fray,[4]
And the wind brings it from the Capitol.

1 ask/request you ("pray you")★
2 only a
3 bustling rumor = agitated clamor/outcry/noise
4 disturbance, quarrel

Lucius Sooth,[5] madam, I hear nothing. 20

ENTER SOOTHSAYER

Portia Come hither, fellow. Which way hast thou been?[6]

Soothsayer At mine own house, good lady.

Portia What is't o'clock?

Soothsayer About the ninth hour, lady.

Portia Is Caesar yet gone to the Capitol?

Soothsayer Madam, not yet. I go to take my stand, 25

To see him pass on to the Capitol.

Portia Thou hast some suit to Caesar, hast thou not?

Soothsayer That I have, lady. If it will please Caesar

To be so good to Caesar as to hear me,

I shall beseech him to befriend himself. 30

Portia Why, know'st thou any harm's intended towards him?

Soothsayer None that I know will be, much that I fear may

chance.

Good morrow to you. Here the street is narrow.

The throng that follows Caesar at the heels,

Of Senators, of Praetors, common suitors, 35

Will crowd a feeble man almost to death.

I'll get me to a place more void,[7] and there

Speak to great Caesar as he comes along.

EXIT SOOTHSAYER

Portia I must go in. Ay me, how weak a thing

The heart of woman is. O Brutus, 40

5 truly, in truth
6 i.e., from where have you just come?
7 more void = emptier

63

The[8] heavens speed thee in thine enterprise!
Sure[9] the boy heard me.[10] Brutus hath a suit
That Caesar will not grant. O, I grow faint.
Run, Lucius, and commend me to my lord,
45 Say I am merry. Come to me again,
And bring me word what he doth say to thee.

EXEUNT

8 may the
9 surely
10 saying "enterprise"

Act 3

SCENE I

Rome, in front of the Capitol

A CROWD, INCLUDING ARTEMIDORUS AND THE SOOTHSAYER

FLOURISH *they're trying to save Caesar*

ENTER CAESAR, BRUTUS, CASSIUS, CASCA, DECIUS
BRUTUS, METELLUS CIMBER, TREBONIUS, CINNA,
ANTONY, LEPIDUS, POPILIUS, PUBLIUS, AND OTHERS

Caesar	(*to Soothsayer*) The Ides of March are come.
Soothsayer	Ay,

Caesar, but not gone.
note
Artemidorus Hail, Caesar! Read this schedule.[1]
Decius Brutus Trebonius doth desire you to o'erread,[2] *best look over*

At your best[3] leisure, this his humble suit. 5
Artemidorus O Caesar, read mine first. For mine's a suit

1 note
2 look over
3 best: a polite, conventional word, adding nothing to the meaning

65

That touches[4] Caesar nearer.[5] Read it, great Caesar.

Caesar   What touches us ourself shall be last served.

Artemidorus Delay not, Caesar, read it instantly.

Caesar   What, is the fellow mad?

Publius   (to Artemidorus) Sirrah,[6]

10   give place.[7]

Cassius   What, urge you your petitions in the street?
       Come to the Capitol.

CAESAR GOES UPSTAGE TO THE SENATE HOUSE,
THE REST FOLLOWING

Popilius   I wish your enterprise today may thrive.[8]

Cassius   What enterprise, Popilius?[9]

Popilius   Fare you well.

15   Brutus   What said Popilius Lena?

Cassius   He wished today our enterprise might thrive.
       I fear our purpose is discoverèd.

Brutus   Look how he makes to[10] Caesar. Mark him.

Cassius   Casca, be sudden,[11] for we fear prevention.

20   Brutus, what shall be done? If this be known,
       Cassius or Caesar never shall turn back,
       For I will slay myself.

Brutus   Cassius, be constant.
       Popilius Lena speaks not of our purposes,

4 affects ("strikes")
5 more closely
6 mister (form of address used in talking down to men)
7 give place = get out of the way
8 prosper, be successful
9 poPILyus
10 makes to = heads for, goes in the direction of
11 quick, speedy

For look he smiles, and Caesar doth not change. *his not telling about our purpose*

Cassius   Trebonius knows his time. For look you, Brutus,   25
He draws Mark Antony out of the way.

EXEUNT ANTONY AND TREBONIUS

Decius Brutus   Where is Metellus Cimber? Let him go,
And presently prefer[12] his suit to Caesar.
Brutus   He is addressed.[13] Press near and second[14] him.
Cinna   Casca, you are the first that rears[15] your hand.   30
Caesar   Are we all ready? What is now amiss
That Caesar and his Senate must redress? *what do we have to change*
Metellus Cimber Most high, most mighty, and most puissant[16]
Caesar,
Metellus Cimber throws before thy seat
An humble heart –

HE KNEELS   *for ordinary men might give*
I should stop you in

Caesar   I must prevent thee, Cimber.   35
These couchings[17] and these lowly courtesies
Might fire the blood of ordinary men,
And turn pre-ordinance[18] and first[19] decree
Into the law[20] of children. Be not fond,[21]

12 presently prefer = now/immediately★ put forward/advance
13 prepared, ready
14 support, assist, back up
15 lifts, raises
16 powerful, potent
17 crouching down, prostrating oneself
18 established rule/law
19 (1) already issued/made/proclaimed, (2) primary
20 Folio: lane; many editors emend
21 foolish, silly

40　To think that Caesar bears such rebel blood[22]
　　That will[23] be thawed[24] from the[25] true quality
　　With[26] that which melteth fools – I mean, sweet words,
　　Low-crookèd[27] court'sies and base spaniel-fawning.
　　Thy brother[28] by decree is banishèd.
45　If thou dost bend and pray and fawn for him,
　　I spurn thee like a cur out of my way.
　　Know, Caesar doth not wrong,[29] nor without cause
　　Will he be satisfied.[30]

Metellus Cimber　Is there no voice more worthy than my own
50　To sound more sweetly in great Caesar's ear
　　For the repealing of my banish'd brother?

Brutus　　　　　I kiss thy hand, but not in flattery, Caesar,
　　Desiring thee that Publius Cimber may
　　Have an immediate freedom of repeal.[31]

Caesar　　　　　What, Brutus?

55　*Cassius*　　　　　Pardon, Caesar. Caesar, pardon.
　　As low as to thy foot doth Cassius fall,
　　To beg enfranchisement[32] for Publius Cimber.

Caesar　　　　　I could be well moved, if I were as[33] you.

---

22 rebel blood = disobedient passions (i.e., in rebellion against the mind/
　reason)
23 he will
24 softened
25 his
26 by means of
27 low-crooked = bowing low
28 Publius Cimber
29 (verb) behave unjustly/unfairly, prejudicially
30 be satisfied = make reparation, meet expectations/desires★
31 freedom of repeal = action of recall from banishment
32 liberation ★
33 like

If I could pray[34] to move, prayers would move me.
But I am constant as the northern star,   60
Of whose true-fixed and resting[35] quality
There is no fellow[36] in the firmament.
The skies are painted with unnumbered sparks,
They are all fire and every one doth shine.
But there's but one in all doth hold his place.   65
So in the world. 'Tis furnished[37] well with men,
And men are flesh and blood, and apprehensive,[38]
Yet in the number I do know but one
That unassailable holds on his rank,[39]
Unshaked of motion. And that I am he,   70
Let me a little[40] show it, even in this.
That I was constant Cimber should be banished,
And constant do remain to keep him so.

Cinna   O Caesar –

Caesar   Hence! Wilt thou lift up Olympus?[41]

Decius Brutus Great Caesar –

Caesar   Doth not Brutus bootless[42] kneel?   75

Casca   Speak hands for me!

CASCA, THEN BRUTUS AND THE OTHER
CONSPIRATORS STAB CAESAR

34 could pray = were capable of asking
35 stationary
36 match, counterpart
37 filled
38 intelligent, discerning
39 position, order
40 in minor things (?), to some extent (?)
41 Mount Olympus
42 in vain

Caesar	Et tu, Brute?[43] Then fall,[44] Caesar.

CAESAR DIES

Cinna	Liberty, freedom! Tyranny is dead!
	Run hence, proclaim, cry it about the streets.
80 *Cassius*	Some to the common pulpits,[45] and cry out
	"Liberty, freedom, and enfranchisement!"
Brutus	People and senators, be not affrighted.
	Fly not, stand still. Ambition's debt is paid.
Casca	Go to the pulpit, Brutus.
Decius Brutus	And Cassius too.
85 *Brutus*	Where's Publius?
Cinna	Here, quite confounded[46] with this mutiny.[47]
Metellus Cimber	Stand fast[48] together, lest some friend of Caesar's
	Should chance –
Brutus	Talk not of standing. Publius, good cheer,
90	There is no harm intended to your person,
	Nor to no Roman else. So tell them, Publius.
Cassius	And leave us, Publius, lest that the people,
	Rushing on us, should do your age some mischief.
Brutus	Do so. And let no man abide[49] this deed,
95	But we the doers.

---

43 and you, Brutus?
44 drop, die
45 platforms★
46 confused, silenced
47 rebellion, revolution★
48 hold fast = stand firm/unshaken
49 (1) remain here, (2) await/expect the consequences, (3) sustain, endure,
  bear★

ENTER TREBONIUS

Cassius   Where is Antony?

Trebonius   Fled to his house amazed.[50]

    Men, wives, and children stare, cry out and run

    As[51] it were doomsday.

Brutus   Fates, we will[52] know your pleasures.

    That we shall die, we know. 'Tis but the time

    And drawing days out, that men stand upon.[53]   100

Cassius   Why, he that cuts off twenty years of life

    Cuts off so many years of fearing death.

Brutus   Grant that, and then is death a benefit.

    So are we Caesar's friends, that have abridged[54]

    His time of fearing death. Stoop Romans, stoop,   105

    And let us bathe our hands in Caesar's blood

    Up to the elbows, and besmear our swords.

    Then walk we forth, even[55] to the marketplace,

    And waving our red weapons o'er our heads,

    Let's all cry "Peace, freedom, and liberty."   110

Cassius   Stoop then, and wash. How many ages hence

    Shall this our lofty scene be acted over

    In states[56] unborn and accents[57] yet unknown!

Brutus   How many times shall Caesar bleed in sport,[58]

---

50 stunned, confused
51 as if
52 wish to
53 stand upon = focus on, emphasize, are concerned with
54 shortened
55 directly
56 Folio: state; all editors emend, as per Second Folio (1632)
57 languages
58 dramatic re-creation

115   That now on Pompey's basis[59] lies along[60]

     No worthier[61] than the dust!

Cassius   So oft as that shall be,

     So often shall the knot[62] of us be called

     The men that gave their country liberty.

Decius Brutus   What, shall we forth?

Cassius   Ay, every man away.

120   Brutus shall lead, and we will grace his heels

     With the most boldest and best hearts of Rome.

ENTER SERVANT

Brutus   Soft. Who comes here? A friend[63] of Antony's.

Servant   (*kneeling*) Thus, Brutus, did my master bid me

     kneel.

     Thus did Mark Antony bid me fall down,

125   And being prostrate, thus he bade me say:

     Brutus is noble, wise, valiant, and honest.

     Caesar was mighty, bold, royal,[64] and loving.

     Say, I love Brutus, and I honor him.

     Say, I feared Caesar, honored him, and loved him.

130   If Brutus will vouchsafe that Antony

     May safely come to him, and be resolved

     How Caesar hath deserved to lie in death,

     Mark Antony shall not love Caesar dead

     So well as Brutus living, but will follow

---

59 pedestal (i.e., of a statue of Pompey)
60 lengthwise, outstretched
61 no worthier = (1) worth no more, (2) no more honorable, esteemed
62 group, band
63 helper, supporter
64 sovereign (adjective), magnificent, munificent

The fortunes and affairs of noble Brutus   135
Thorough[65] the hazards[66] of this untrod[67] state,
With all true faith. So says my master Antony.
Brutus   Thy master is a wise and valiant Roman,
I never thought him worse.
Tell him, so please him come unto this place   140
He shall be satisfied and, by my honor,
Depart untouched.
Servant   I'll fetch him presently.

EXIT SERVANT

Brutus   I know that we shall have him well to[68] friend.
Cassius   I wish we may. But yet have I a mind
That fears him much. And my misgiving still[69]   145
Falls shrewdly to the purpose.[70]
Brutus   But here comes Antony.

ENTER ANTONY

Welcome, Mark Antony.
Antony   O mighty Caesar! Dost thou lie so low?
Are all thy conquests, glories, triumphs, spoils,[71]
Shrunk to this little measure?[72] Fare thee well.   150

65 through
66 risks, ventures, chances★
67 as yet uncertain
68 as a
69 misgiving still = misgivings always
70 falls shrewdly to the purpose = occurs/comes down★ sharply/intensely on
   target/to the point
71 booty, loot★
72 length

I know not, gentlemen, what you intend,
Who else must be let blood, who else is rank.[73]
If I myself, there is no hour so fit
As Caesar's death hour, nor no instrument
155 Of half that worth as those your swords, made rich
With the most noble blood of all this world.
I do beseech ye, if you bear me hard,
Now, whilst your purpled hands do reek[74] and smoke,[75]
Fulfill[76] your pleasure. Live[77] a thousand years,
160 I shall not find myself so apt to die.
No place will please me so, no mean[78] of death,
As here by Caesar, and by you cut off,
The choice and master spirits of this age.

Brutus O Antony, beg not your death of us.
165 Though now we must appear bloody and cruel,
As by our hands, and this our present act,
You see we do, yet see you but our hands,
And this, the bleeding business they have done.
Our hearts you see not, they are pitiful.[79]
170 And pity to[80] the general wrong of Rome –
As fire drives out fire, so pity, pity –
Hath done this deed on Caesar. For your part,
To you our swords have leaden points, Mark Antony:

[handwritten marginal note:] basically, he's saying at how a man so great at felsoearily, Kill me now, by the corpse of my friend

73 (1) loathsome, (2) swollen, overgrown (i.e., requiring medicinal bloodletting)
74 steam
75 send off vapor
76 satisfy, complete, carry out
77 if I live
78 means
79 compassionate, merciful, tender
80 for

Our arms in strength of malice,[81] and our hearts
Of brothers' temper, do receive you in   175
With all kind love, good thoughts, and reverence.[82]

Cassius Your voice shall be as strong as any man's
In the disposing[83] of new dignities.[84]

Brutus Only be patient, till we have appeased[85]
The multitude, beside themselves with fear,   180
And then we will deliver[86] you the cause
Why I, that did love Caesar when I struck him, ←   *I wonder why Brutus killed him*
Have thus proceeded.

Antony   I doubt not of your wisdom.
Let each man render me his bloody hand.
First Marcus Brutus will I shake with you.   185
Next Caius Cassius do I take your hand.
Now Decius Brutus yours. Now yours Metellus.
Yours Cinna. And my valiant Casca, yours.   *Wait and we will tell you*
Though last, not last in love, yours good Treb̲o̲n̲i̲u̲s̲.   *he wasn't bloody why we killed him*
Gentlemen all. Alas, what shall I say?   190
My credit[87] now stands on such slippery ground
That one of two bad ways you must conceit me,
Either a coward or a flatterer.
That I did love thee Caesar, O 'tis true.   *I really did love you*
If then thy spirit look upon us now,   195
Shall it not grieve thee dearer than thy death

81 violence, hatred
82 respect, deference★
83 arrangement, awarding
84 IN the disPOSing OF new DIGnitTIES
85 pacified, quieted
86 express, speak
87 trustworthiness, credibility

To see thy thy Antony making his peace,
Shaking the bloody fingers of thy foes –
Most noble! – in the presence of thy corse?[88]

200   Had I as many eyes as thou hast wounds,
Weeping as fast as they stream forth thy blood,
It would become[89] me better than to close[90]
In terms of friendship with thine enemies.
Pardon me, Julius! Here wast thou bayed,[91] brave hart,[92]

205   Here didst thou fall, and here thy hunters stand,
Signed[93] in thy spoil,[94] and crimsoned in thy lethe.[95]
O world, thou wast the forest to this hart,
And this indeed, O world, the heart of thee.
How like a deer, strucken by many princes,

210   Dost thou here lie!

  Cassius Mark Antony –

  Antony   Pardon me, Caius Cassius.
The enemies of Caesar shall say this.[96]
Then,[97] in a friend it is cold modesty.[98]

  Cassius I blame you not for praising Caesar so,

215   But what compact[99] mean you to have with us?

88 corpse
89 suit, fit
90 unite, join
91 stood at bay, surrounded*
92 (1) stag, male deer, (2) heart
93 marked
94 (1) damaging, spoiling, (2) dead body
95 death (the river of forgetting life, marking the entrance to Lethe / Hades:
   LEEthee)
96 i.e, the praise / respect Antony has shown Caesar
97 accordingly
98 self-control / moderation
99 agreement, understanding ("contract")

Will you be pricked[100] in number of our friends,
Or shall we on,[101] and not depend on you?

Antony   Therefore I took your hands, but was indeed
Swayed[102] from the point, by looking down on Caesar.
Friends am I with you all, and love you all,   220
Upon this hope,[103] that you shall give me reasons
Why, and wherein, Caesar was dangerous.

Brutus   Or else were this a savage spectacle.
Our reasons are so full of good regard
That were you, Antony, the son of Caesar,   225
You should be satisfied.

Antony   That's all I seek.
And am moreover suitor that I may
Produce[104] his body to the marketplace,
And in[105] the pulpit, as becomes a friend,
Speak in the order[106] of his funeral.   230

Brutus   You shall, Mark Antony.

Cassius   Brutus, a word with you.
(*aside to Brutus*) You know not what you do. Do not consent
That Antony speak in his funeral
Know you how much the people may be moved
By that which he will utter?

Brutus   By your pardon.[107]   235

100   written, recorded★
101   proceed on
102   diverted, moved
103   (1) expectation, (2) desire, wish
104   bring (to view)
105   on
106   arrangement ("sequence")
107   by your pardon = with your permission, excuse me

I will myself into[108] the pulpit first,

And show the reason of our Caesar's death.

What Antony shall speak, I will protest[109]   *declare*

He speaks by leave and by permission,[110]

240   And that we are contented Caesar shall

Have all true rites and lawful ceremonies.

It shall advantage[111] more, than do us wrong.

Cassius I know not what may fall, I like it not.

Brutus Mark Antony, here take you Caesar's body.

245   You shall[112] not in your funeral speech blame us,

But speak all good you can devise[113] of Caesar,

And say you do't by our permission,

Else shall you not have any hand at all

About his funeral. And you shall speak

250   In the same pulpit whereto I am going,

After[114] my speech is ended.

Antony   Be it so.

I do desire no more.

Brutus Prepare the body then, and follow us.

EXEUNT ALL BUT ANTONY

Antony O, pardon me, thou bleeding piece of earth,

255   That I am meek and gentle with these butchers!

Thou art the ruins of the noblest man

108 go onto
109 declare, affirm
110 perMIseeOWN
111 (verb) profit, gain
112 must
113 (1) think, (2) invent
114 and you will speak after

That ever lived in the tide[115] of times.
Woe to the hand that shed this costly[116] blood!
Over thy wounds now do I prophesy
(Which[117] like dumb mouths do ope their ruby lips,   260
To beg the voice and utterance of my tongue)
A curse shall light upon the limbs of men,
Domestic[118] fury and fierce civil strife
Shall cumber[119] all the parts of Italy.
Blood and destruction shall be so in use   265
And dreadful objects so familiar
That mothers shall but smile when they behold
Their infants quartered[120] with the hands of war,
All pity choked with custom[121] of fell[122] deeds,
And Caesar's spirit ranging for revenge,   270
With Ate[123] by his side come hot from hell,
Shall in these confines[124] with a monarch's voice
Cry havoc,[125] and let slip[126] the dogs of war,
That[127] this foul deed shall smell above the earth
With carrion men,[128] groaning for burial.   275

115 recurrent flow
116 sumptuous, of great value
117 your wounds which
118 internal to the Romans
119 harass, burden, overwhelm
120 cut into four parts
121 the habit, usual practice
122 cruel, savage, ruthless
123 goddess of mischief / rash destructive actions (AYtee: rhymes with "Haiti")
124 in these confines = (1) within / inside these borders / boundaries / frontiers,
    (2) in these territories / regions
125 order signaling an army to begin pillage / looting
126 let slip = unleash
127 so that
128 carrion men = corpses of human beings

ENTER SERVANT

You serve Octavius Caesar, do you not?

Servant I do, Mark Antony.

Antony Caesar did write for him to come to Rome.

Servant He did receive his letters, and is coming,

280   And bid me say to you by word of mouth –

    (*sees the corpse*) O Caesar! –

Antony Thy heart is big.[129] Get thee apart[130] and weep. *Crying overwhelmed*

    Passion I see is catching, for[131] mine eyes,

    Seeing those beads of sorrow stand in thine,

285   Began to water. Is thy master coming? *Seven is 21 miles*

Servant He lies tonight within seven leagues[132] of Rome. *from Rome*

Antony Post[133] back with speed, and tell him what hath

    chanced. *Tell him what happened, so he won't come*

    Here is a mourning Rome, a dangerous Rome, *until the crowd is*

    No Rome of safety for Octavius yet. *calm*

290   Hie hence, and tell him so. Yet stay awhile, *Rome is like really*

    Thou shalt not back[134] till I have borne this corse *dangerous for*

    Into the marketplace. There shall I try[135] *Octavios, Caesars*

    In my oration, how the people take *adopted son...*

    The cruel issue[136] of these bloody men,

129 (1) stout, great, (2) swollen
130 to one side
131 Folio: from; all editors emend
132 21 miles (1 league = 3 miles)
133 ride, travel
134 go back
135 test
136 proceeding, action

According to the which,[137] thou shalt discourse[138]   295
To young Octavius of the state of things.
Lend me your hand.

EXEUNT WITH CAESAR'S BODY

137 i.e., how the "test" goes
138 speak

SCENE 2

Rome, the Forum

ENTER BRUTUS, CASSIUS, AND PLEBEIANS

Plebeians	We will[1] be satisfied! Let us be satisfied!
Brutus	Then follow me, and give me audience,[2] friends.

Cassius, go you into the other street,

And part the numbers.[3]

5   Those that will hear me speak, let 'em stay here;

Those that will follow Cassius, go with him,

And public[4] reasons shall be rendered

Of Caesar's death. *We will publically tell them why we killed him*

First Plebeian   I will hear Brutus speak.

Second Plebeian   I will hear Cassius, and compare their reasons,

10   When severally we hear[5] them rendered.

EXIT CASSIUS, WITH SOME PLEBEIANS

BRUTUS GOES TO THE PULPIT

Third Plebeian   The noble Brutus is ascended. Silence!

Brutus   Be patient till the last.

Romans, countrymen, and lovers, hear me for my cause, and

be silent, that you may hear. Believe me for mine honor, and

15   have respect to mine honor, that you may believe. Censure

me in your wisdom, and awake your senses, that you may the

better judge.

---

1 wish/want to
2 give me audience = listen to me★
3 part the numbers = divide the crowd
4 open to/in the presence of all the community
5 have heard

If there be any in this assembly, any dear friend of Caesar's,
to him I say that Brutus' love to Caesar was no less than his.
If then that friend demand why Brutus rose against Caesar,   20
this is my answer: Not that I loved Caesar less, but that I loved
Rome more. Had[6] you rather Caesar were living and die all
slaves, than that Caesar were dead, to live all free men? As
Caesar loved me, I weep for him; as he was fortunate, I rejoice
at it; as he was valiant, I honor him. But as he was ambitious,   25
I slew him. There is tears for his love; joy for his fortune;
honor for his valor; and death for his ambition. Who is here
so base that would be a bondman? If any, speak, for him have
I offended. Who is here so rude that would not be a Roman?
If any, speak, for him have I offended. Who is here so vile that   30
will not love his country? If any, speak, for him have I
offended. I pause for a reply.

All   None, Brutus, none.

Brutus Then none have I offended. I have done no more to
Caesar than you shall do to Brutus. The question[7] of his   35
death is enrolled[8] in the Capitol, his glory not extenuated,[9]
wherein he was worthy, nor his offenses enforced,[10] for
which he suffered death.

ENTER ANTONY AND OTHERS, WITH CAESAR'S BODY

Here comes his body, mourned by Mark Antony, who though
he had no hand in his death, shall receive the benefit of his[11]   40

6 would
7 subject, facts
8 inscribed, recorded
9 shrunken, diminished, reduced
10 emphasized, asserted, pressed
11 Caesar's

83

dying, a place in the commonwealth, as which of you shall
not? With this[12] I depart – that, as I slew my best lover for
the good of Rome, I have the same dagger for myself, when
it shall please my country to need my death.

45 *All*   Live Brutus, live, live!

First Plebeian   Bring him with triumph home unto his house.

Second Plebeian Give him a statue with his ancestors.

Third Plebeian   Let him be Caesar.

Fourth Plebeian   Caesar's better parts[13]

Shall be crowned in Brutus.

First Plebeian   We'll bring him to his house

50 With shouts and clamors.

Brutus   My countrymen –

Second Plebeian   Peace, silence, Brutus speaks.

First Plebeian   Peace, ho!

Brutus   Good countrymen, let me depart alone,

And (for my sake) stay here with Antony.

55 Do grace to Caesar's corpse, and grace his speech
Tending to[14] Caesar's glories, which Mark Antony,
By our permission, is allowed to make.
I do entreat you, not a man depart,
Save I alone, till Antony have spoke.

EXIT BRUTUS

60 *First Plebeian*   Stay ho, and let us hear Mark Antony.

Third Plebeian   Let him go up into the public chair,[15]

---

12 word
13 characteristics, capabilities, talents
14 tending to = dealing with
15 place/location of authority

We'll hear him. Noble Antony, go up.

Antony   For Brutus' sake, I am beholding[16] to you.

GOES TO PULPIT

Fourth Plebeian What does he say of Brutus?

Third Plebeian He says, for Brutus' sake,   65

  He finds himself beholding to us all.

Fourth Plebeian 'Twere best he speak no harm of Brutus here.

First Plebeian This Caesar was a tyrant.

Third Plebeian   Nay, that's certain.

  We are blest that Rome is rid of him.

Second Plebeian Peace, let us hear what Antony can say.   70

Antony   You gentle Romans –

Plebeians   Peace, ho, let us hear him.

Antony   Friends, Romans, countrymen, lend me your

  ears. *[Common wall]*

  I come to bury Caesar, not to praise him.

  The evil that men do lives after them,

  The good is oft interrèd[17] with their bones.   75

  So let it be with Caesar. The noble Brutus

  Hath told you Caesar was ambitious.[18] *they're honorable*

  If it were so, it was a grievous fault, *although*

  And grievously hath Caesar answered[19] it. *they killed*

  Here, under leave of Brutus, and the rest *Caesar*   80

  (For Brutus is an honorable man,

  So are they all, all honorable men)

16 obliged, indebted
17 buried
18 amBIseeUS
19 been held responsible for

Come I to speak in[20] Caesar's funeral.
He was my friend, faithful and just to me.
85 But Brutus says he was ambitious,
And Brutus is an honorable man.
He hath brought many captives home to Rome,
Whose ransoms did the general coffers fill.
Did this in Caesar seem ambitious?
90 When that the poor have cried, Caesar hath wept.
Ambition should be made of sterner[21] stuff.
Yet Brutus says he was ambitious.
And Brutus is an honorable man.
You all did see that on[22] the Lupercal
95 I thrice presented him a kingly crown,
Which he did thrice refuse. Was this ambition?
Yet Brutus says he was ambitious,
And sure[23] he is an honorable man.
I speak not to disprove what Brutus spoke,
100 But here I am to speak what I do know.
You all did love him once, not without cause.
What cause withholds you then, to mourn for him?
O judgment![24] Thou art fled to brutish beasts,
And men have lost their reason. Bear with me,
105 My heart is in the coffin there with Caesar,
And I must pause till it come back to me.
First Plebeian Methinks there is much reason in his sayings.

20 at
21 more rigorous, less flexible
22 at the time of
23 surely
24 discernment, reasonable opinion / estimate / valuation

Second Plebeian If thou consider rightly of the matter,

  Caesar has had great wrong.

Third Plebeian   Has he, masters?[25]

  I fear there will a worse come in his place.   110

Fourth Plebeian Marked ye his words? He would not take the
  crown,

  Therefore 'tis certain he was not ambitious.

First Plebeian   If it be found so, some will dear abide it.

Second Plebeian Poor soul,[26] his eyes are red as fire with
  weeping.

Third Plebeian   There's not a nobler man in Rome than Antony. 115

Fourth Plebeian Now mark him, he begins again to speak.

Antony   But yesterday the word of Caesar might

  Have stood against the world. Now lies he there,

  And none so poor to do[27] him reverence.

  O masters! If I were disposed to stir   120

  Your hearts and minds to mutiny and rage,

  I should do Brutus wrong, and Cassius wrong,

  Who (you all know) are honorable men.

  I will not do them wrong. I rather choose

  To wrong the dead, to wrong myself and you,   125

  Than I will wrong such honorable men.

  But here's a parchment,[28] with the seal of Caesar.

  I found it in his closet, 'tis his will.

  Let but the commons[29] hear this testament[30]

25 fellows (the plebeian counterpart to "gentlemen")
26 i.e., Antony
27 so poor to do = so poor that they do
28 document
29 common / ordinary people
30 will ("declaration")

87

130 (Which pardon me, I do not mean to read)
    And they would go and kiss dead Caesar's wounds
    And dip their napkins[31] in his sacred blood,
    Yea, beg a hair of him for memory
    And, dying, mention it within their wills,
135 Bequeathing it as a rich legacy
    Unto their issue.[32]

Fourth Plebeian We'll hear the will. Read it, Mark Antony.

All   The will, the will! We will hear Caesar's will.

Antony   Have patience, gentle friends, I must not read it,
140 It is not meet you know how Caesar loved you.
    You are not wood, you are not stones, but men.
    And being men, hearing the will of Caesar,
    It will inflame you, it will make you mad.
    'Tis good you know not[33] that you are his heirs,
145 For if you should, O what would come of it?

Fourth Plebeian Read the will, we'll hear it, Antony.
    You shall[34] read us the will, Caesar's will.

Antony   Will you be patient? Will you stay[35] awhile?
    I have o'ershot[36] myself to tell you of it,
150 I fear I wrong the honorable men
    Whose daggers have stabbed Caesar. I do fear it.

Fourth Plebeian They were traitors. Honorable men?

All   The will! the testament!

---

31 handkerchiefs, small towels, etc.
32 children
33 know not = do not know
34 must
35 wait
36 exceeded, gone beyond/too far

Second Plebeian	They were villains, murderers. The will, read the will.
Antony	You will compel me, then, to read the will? 155

Then make a ring about the corpse of Caesar,

And let me show you him that made the will.

Shall I descend? And will you give me leave?

Several Plebeians Come down.

Second Plebeian   Descend.

Third Plebeian   You shall have leave.

ANTONY COMES DOWN

Fourth Plebeian A ring, stand round.   160

First Plebeian Stand from[37] the hearse,[38] stand from the
body.

Second Plebeian Room for Antony, most noble Antony.

Antony Nay press not so upon me, stand far[39] off.

Several Plebeians Stand back. Room, bear[40] back.

Antony If you have tears, prepare to shed them now.   165

You all do know this mantle.[41] I remember

The first time ever Caesar put it on.

'Twas on a summer's evening, in his tent,

That day he overcame the Nervii.[42]

Look, in this place ran Cassius' dagger through.   170

See what a rent[43] the envious Casca made.

37 away from
38 coffin, bier
39 further
40 move, push
41 cloak
42 57 B.C.: a fierce Belgic tribe (NERveeEYE)
43 fissure, cleft

Through this the well-belovèd Brutus stabbed,
And as he plucked his cursèd steel away,
Mark how the blood of Caesar followed it,
175   As[44] rushing out of doors, to be resolved[45]
If Brutus so unkindly[46] knocked,[47] or no.
For Brutus, as you know, was Caesar's angel.[48]
Judge, O you gods, how dearly Caesar loved him!
This was the most unkindest cut of all.
180   For when the noble Caesar saw him stab,
Ingratitude, more strong than traitors' arms,
Quite vanquished him. Then burst his mighty heart,
And in his mantle muffling up his face,
Even at the base of Pompey's statue
185   (Which all the while ran blood), great Caesar fell.
O what a fall was there, my countrymen!
Then I, and you, and all of us fell down,
Whilst bloody treason flourished[49] over us.
O now you weep, and I perceive you feel
190   The dint[50] of pity. These are gracious drops.
Kind souls, what! Weep you when you but behold
Our Caesar's vesture[51] wounded? Look you here,
Here is himself, marred[52] as you see with[53] traitors.

44 as if
45 convinced, satisfied, settled, decided
46 (1) unnaturally, cruelly, (2) ungratefully
47 (1) struck, hit hard, (2) rapped (as on a door)
48 shining/lovely person
49 thrived, flowered
50 (1) stroke, blow, attack, (2) impact, impression, mark
51 clothing
52 damaged, harmed, destroyed, ruined
53 by

First Plebeian	O piteous spectacle!
Second Plebeian	O noble Caesar!	195
Third Plebeian	O woeful day!
Fourth Plebeian	O traitors, villains!
First Plebeian	O most bloody sight!
Second Plebeian	We will be revenged.
All	Revenge! About![54] Seek! Burn! Fire! Kill! Slay! 200

Let not a traitor live!

Antony   Stay, countrymen.

First Plebeian   Peace there! Hear the noble Antony.

Second Plebeian We'll hear him, we'll follow him, we'll die with
him.

Antony   Good friends, sweet friends, let me not stir you up 205
To such a sudden flood of mutiny.
They that have done this deed are honorable.
What private griefs they have, alas I know not,
That made them do it. They are wise and honorable,
And will no doubt with reasons answer you.   210
I come not, friends, to steal away your hearts,
I am no orator, as Brutus is,
But (as you know me all) a plain blunt man
That love my friend, and that they know full well
That[55] gave me public leave to speak of him.   215
For I have neither writ,[56] nor words, nor worth,
Action,[57] nor utterance,[58] nor the power of speech,

54 let's go
55 those who
56 a prepared/written speech; Second Folio (1632) has "wit," to which some
editors emend
57 acting ability, gestures
58 fluency

To stir men's blood.[59] I only speak right on.

I tell you that which you yourselves do know,

220 Show you sweet Caesar's wounds, poor poor dumb mouths,

And bid them speak for me But were I Brutus,

And Brutus[60] Antony, there[61] were an Antony

Would ruffle[62] up your spirits, and put a tongue

In every wound of Caesar that should move

225 The stones of Rome to rise and mutiny.

All	We'll mutiny.
First Plebeian	We'll burn the house of Brutus.
Third Plebeian	Away, then, come, seek the conspirators.
Antony	Yet hear me countrymen, yet hear me speak.
All	Peace, ho! Hear Antony, most noble Antony.

230 *Antony*   Why friends, you go to do you know not what.

Wherein hath Caesar thus deserved your loves?

Alas you know not, I must tell you then.

You have forgot the will I told you of.

All   Most true, the will, let's stay and hear the will.

235 *Antony*   Here is the will, and under Caesar's seal.

To every Roman citizen he gives –

To every several man – seventy-five drachmas.[63]

Second Plebeian Most noble Caesar! We'll revenge his death.

Third Plebeian O royal Caesar!

Antony   Hear me with patience.

All   Peace,

ho!

59 passions, emotions★
60 and Brutus = and if Brutus were
61 (heavily emphasized)
62 stir
63 silver coins (DRACKmas): 75 drachmas = 3/4 lb. silver

Antony	Moreover, he hath left you all his walks,	240

His private arbors[64] and new-planted orchards,

On this side Tiber.[65] He hath left them you,

And to your heirs for ever, common pleasures,

To walk abroad, and recreate[66] yourselves.

Here was a Caesar. When comes such another?   245

First Plebeian   Never, never. Come, away, away!

We'll burn his body in the holy place,

And with the brands[67] fire the traitors' houses.

Take[68] up the body.

Second Plebeian Go fetch fire.   250

Third Plebeian   Pluck[69] down benches.

Fourth Plebeian Pluck down forms,[70] windows, anything.

EXEUNT PLEBEIANS WITH THE BODY

Antony   Now let it work. Mischief, thou art afoot,

Take thou what course thou wilt!

ENTER SERVANT

How now, fellow!

Servant   Sir, Octavius is already come to Rome.   255

Antony   Where is he?

Servant   He and Lepidus[71] are at Caesar's house.

Antony   And thither will I straight to visit him.

64 bowers (shaded resting places)
65 side Tiber = side of the Tiber River
66 reinvigorate, restore, refresh (REKreeATE)
67 glowing sticks
68 lift
69 pull
70 images, statues
71 LEpiDUS

He comes upon a wish.[72] Fortune is merry,

260   And in this mood will give us anything.

Servant I heard him say, Brutus and Cassius

Are rid[73] like madmen through the gates of Rome.

Antony Belike[74] they had some notice[75] of the people,

How I had moved them. Bring me to Octavius.

EXEUNT

72 upon a wish = according to a/my wish
73 are ride = have ridden
74 probably, perhaps
75 warning, information

SCENE 3

Rome, a street

ENTER CINNA THE POET

Poet   I dreamt tonight that I did feast with Caesar,
And things unluckily charge[1] my fantasy.
I have no will[2] to wander forth of doors,[3]
Yet something leads me forth.

ENTER PLEBEIANS

First Plebeian	What is your name?	5
Second Plebeian	Whither are you going?	
Third Plebeian	Where do you dwell?	
Fourth Plebeian	Are you a married man or a bachelor?	
Second Plebeian	Answer every man directly.	
First Plebeian	Ay, and briefly.	10
Fourth Plebeian	Ay, and wisely.	
Third Plebeian	Ay, and truly, you were best.[4]	

Poet   What is my name? Whither am I going? Where
do I dwell? Am I a married man or a bachelor? Then, to
answer every man directly and briefly, wisely and truly. 15
Wisely I say, I am a bachelor.

Second Plebeian That's as much as to say, they are fools that
marry. You'll bear me a bang for that, I fear. Proceed, directly.

Poet   Directly, I am going to Caesar's funeral.

First Plebeian   As a friend or an enemy? 20

---

1 fill, load, burden
2 desire
3 forth of doors = abroad
4 you were best = you had better

Poet	As a friend.
Second Plebeian	That matter is answered directly.
Fourth Plebeian	For your dwelling: briefly.
Poet	Briefly, I dwell by the Capitol.
25 *Third Plebeian*	Your name, sir, truly.
Poet	Truly, my name is Cinna.
First Plebeian	Tear him to pieces, he's a conspirator.
Poet	I am Cinna the poet, I am Cinna the poet!
Fourth Plebeian	Tear him for his bad verses, tear him for his bad verses.
30 *Poet*	I am not Cinna the conspirator!
Fourth Plebeian	It is no matter, his name's Cinna. Pluck but his name out of his heart, and turn him going.[5]
Third Plebeian	Tear him, tear him! Come, brands, ho fire-brands! To Brutus', to Cassius', burn all! Some to Decius'
35	house, and some to Casca's, some to Ligarius'! Away, go!

EXEUNT

5 i.e., to his grave, along with Caesar

96

Act 4

SCENE I

A house in Rome

ANTONY, OCTAVIUS, AND LEPIDUS, SEATED AT A TABLE

Antony These many, then, shall[1] die, their names are pricked.

Octavius Your brother too must die. Consent you, Lepidus?

Lepidus I do consent.

Octavius Prick him down, Antony.

Lepidus Upon condition Publius shall not live,   5

Who is your sister's son, Mark Antony.

Antony He shall not live. Look, with a spot I damn him.

But Lepidus, go you to Caesar's house.

Fetch the will hither, and we shall determine[2]

How to cut off[3] some charge[4] in legacies.   10

Lepidus What? Shall I find you here?

1 must
2 decide★
3 away, out
4 cost, expense

97

Octavius Or[5] here, or at the Capitol.

EXIT LEPIDUS

Antony This is a slight unmeritable[6] man, [*untrustworthy*]

Meet to be sent on errands. Is it fit,

15   The threefold world[7] divided, he should stand[8]

One of the three to share it?   [*should all three of us rule?*]

Octavius   So you thought him,

And took his voice who should be pricked to die [*i.e., you think? yeah*]

In our black[9] sentence and proscription.[10]

Antony Octavius, I have seen more days than you,

20   And though we lay these honors on this man

To ease ourselves of divers slanderous[11] loads,

He shall but bear them as the ass bears gold,

To groan and sweat under the business,

Either led or driven, as we point the way.

25   And having brought[12] our treasure[13] where we will,[14]

Then take we down his load, and turn him off[15]

(Like to the empty[16] ass) to shake his ears,

[*Lepidus = donkey*]   [*donkey*]

[*Octavius is Caesar's adopted son*]   [*Antony & Octavius struggle for power*]

5 either
6 undeserving, unworthy (unMEriTAble)
7 threefold world = Europe, Asia, Africa (N. and S. America and Australia were unknown to the Romans)
8 remain, stay
9 gloomy, foul, deadly (adjective modifying both "sentence" and "proscription")
10 sentence and proscription = judgment/decision and banishment/outlawing (proSCRIPseeOWN)★
11 divers slanderous = various/different shameful/disgraceful
12 i.e., having had it carried by Lepidus/the donkey
13 i.e., a reference back to "gold"
14 wish it to be
15 turn him off = dismiss/discharge him, send him away
16 unloaded

And graze in commons.[17]

Octavius   You may do your will.[18]

But he's a tried[19] and valiant soldier.

Antony   So is my horse, Octavius, and for that   30

I do appoint[20] him store of provender.[21]

It is a creature that I teach to fight,

To wind,[22] to stop, to run directly on,

His corporal[23] motion governed by my spirit,

And in some taste[24] is Lepidus but so.   35

He must be taught, and trained, and bid go forth,

A barren-spirited fellow, one that feeds

On objects, arts, and imitations,[25]

Which out of use and staled[26] by other men

Begin his fashion.[27] Do not talk of him   40

But as a property.[28] And now Octavius,

Listen[29] great things. Brutus and Cassius

Are levying powers.[30] We must straight make head.[31]

17 in commons = on public pastureland

18 do your will = do as you wish

19 tested, proven, experienced

20 provide for

21 store of provender = a sufficient / abundant supply of food / fodder

22 turn (rhymes with "mind," "kind," etc.)

23 bodily, physical

24 sense, way

25 objects, arts, and imitations = (1) things, (2) goals / purposes, skills / workmanship, and (1) outward forms, (2) copying / imitating (ImiTAYseeOWNZ)

26 out of use and staled = being used and worn out

27 style, pattern, mode, methods (i.e., he barely starts at the point where other / better men have already been and gone)

28 possession

29 listen / pay attention to

30 troops, armies★

31 make head = get started / advance in matters of war (also means " attack")

Therefore let our alliance be combined,[32]
45 Our best friends made,[33] our means stretched,[34]
And let us presently go sit in council
How covert[35] matters may be best disclosed,
And open[36] perils surest[37] answered.

Octavius Let us do so. For we are at the stake,[38]
50 And bayed about with many enemies,
And some that smile have in their hearts I fear
Millions of mischiefs.

EXEUNT

32 i.e., operate as one
33 solicited, contacted
34 used to the full
35 secret, hidden
36 clear, obvious
37 most safely/securely
38 post to which a captive bear was chained, to be set upon by dogs ("bearbaiting")

SCENE 2

Camp near Sardis,[1] *in front of Brutus' tent*

DRUMS

ENTER BRUTUS, LUCILIUS, LUCIUS, AND SOLDIERS

TITINIUS AND PINDARUS APPROACH THEM
FROM THE OTHER SIDE OF THE STAGE

Brutus   Stand, ho.[2]

Lucilius   Give the word,[3] ho, and stand.

Brutus   What now Lucilius, is Cassius near?

Lucilius   He is at hand, and Pindarus[4] is come

To do you salutation[5] from his master.[6]

Brutus   He greets me well. Your master, Pindarus,   5

In his own change,[7] or by ill[8] officers,

Hath given me some worthy[9] cause to wish

Things done,[10] undone. But if he be at hand

I shall be satisfied.

Pindarus   I do not doubt

But that my noble master will appear[11]   10

Such as he is, full of regard[12] and honor.

1 city in Asia Minor (the Near East)
2 halt, stop
3 speak
4 PINdaRUS
5 honor, greeting
6 Cassius
7 substitutions, changes
8 blameworthy, bad
9 good, strong, significant
10 things done = things that had been done
11 show himself
12 concern, attentiveness

Brutus   He is not doubted.

PINDARUS STEPS ASIDE

A word, Lucilius.

How he received you, let me be resolved.

Lucilius   With courtesy and with respect enough,

15   But not with such familiar instances,[13]

Nor with such free and friendly conference[14]

As he hath used of old.

Brutus   Thou hast described

A hot friend cooling. Ever note, Lucilius,

When love[15] begins to sicken and decay

20   It useth an enforcèd ceremony.[16]

There are no tricks, in plain and simple faith.

But hollow men, like horses hot at hand,[17]

Make gallant show and promise of their mettle.

DRUMS IN THE DISTANCE, COMING CLOSER

But when they should[18] endure the bloody spur,

25   They fall their crests,[19] and like deceitful jades[20]

Sink[21] in the trial. Comes his army on?[22]

Lucilius   They mean this night in Sardis to be quartered.

---

13 familiar instances = friendly/intimate signs
14 conversation
15 regard, friendship
16 enforcèd ceremony = constrained/labored politeness/courtesy
17 hot at hand = excited/eager at the start
18 must
19 surface line of a horse's neck
20 worthless/worn-out horses
21 give way, burn out
22 comes … on = arrives

The greater part, the horse[23] in general,

Are[24] come with Cassius.

Brutus   Hark, he is[25] arrived.

March gently[26] on to meet him.   30

ENTER CASSIUS AND SOLDIERS

Cassius   Stand, ho!

Brutus   Stand, ho! Speak the word along.

First Soldier   Stand!

Second Soldier Stand!

Third Soldier   Stand!   35

Cassius   Most noble brother, you have done me wrong.

Brutus   Judge me, you gods. Wrong I mine enemies?[27]

And if not so, how should I wrong a brother?

Cassius   Brutus, this sober[28] form of yours hides wrongs,

And when you do them —

Brutus   Cassius, be content.   40

Speak your griefs softly: I do know you well.

Before the eyes of both our armies here,

Which should perceive nothing but love from us,

Let us not wrangle.[29] Bid them move away.

Then in my tent, Cassius, enlarge[30] your griefs,   45

And I will give you audience.

23 cavalry

24 have

25 has

26 (1) courteously, (2) slowly

27 wrong I mine enemies? = do I injure (even) my enemies?

28 moderate, temperate

29 quarrel / argue / dispute loudly / vehemently

30 amplify, expand

Cassius   Pindarus, ~~take the troops away~~

    Bid our commanders lead their charges[31] off

    A little from this ground.   he agreed

Brutus Lucilius, do you the like, and let no man

50   Come to our tent till we have done our conference.

    Let Lucius and Titinius guard our door.[32]

EXEUNT

31 soldiers they lead/are in charge of
32 let LOOshus AND tiTINyus GUARD our DOOR

ACT 4 • SCENE 3

SCENE 3

Brutus' tent

ENTER BRUTUS AND CASSIUS

Cassius That you have wronged me doth appear in this:
You have condemned and noted[1] Lucius Pella
For taking bribes here of[2] the Sardians,[3]
Wherein[4] my letters, praying[5] on his side
(Because I knew the man), was[6] slighted off.[7]
Brutus You wronged yourself to write in such a case.
Cassius In such a time as this it is not meet

That every nice[8] offense should bear his comment.[9]

Brutus Let me tell you Cassius, you yourself
Are much condemned to have an itching palm,   10
To sell and mart[10] your offices for gold
To undeservers.

Cassius   I, an itching palm!

You know[11] that you are Brutus that speaks this,
Or by the gods, this speech were else your last.

Brutus The name of Cassius honors this corruption,   15
And chastisement[12] doth therefore hide his head.

---

1 indicted, branded, singled out
2 from
3 inhabitants of Sardis
4 in which matter
5 petitioning, entreating
6 letters . . . was: acceptable usage in Shakespeare's time
7 slighted off = put aside, disregarded, disdained
8 (1) particular, precise, (2) slight, small
9 bear his comment = carry/endure its criticism
10 make merchandise of, traffic in
11 had better believe
12 punishment, discipline, correction (CHAStizeMENT)

Cassius Chastisement!

Brutus Remember March, the Ides of March remember.
Did not great Julius bleed for justice[13] sake?
20 What villain touched his body, that did stab
And not[14] for justice? What? Shall one of us,
That struck the foremost man of all this world,
But[15] for supporting[16] robbers shall we now
Contaminate our fingers with base bribes,
25 And sell the mighty space[17] of our large honors[18]
For so much trash[19] as may be graspèd thus?
I had rather be a dog, and bay[20] the moon,
Than such a Roman.

Cassius   Brutus, bait[21] not me,
I'll not endure it. You forget yourself
30 To hedge me in. I am a soldier, I,
Older in practice,[22] abler[23] than yourself
To make conditions.[24]

Brutus   Go to.[25] You are not, Cassius.

Cassius I am.

13 modern syntax requires an apostrophe, here, and in similar cases I have
   supplied one. But to modernize Folio "justice" to "justice's" seems to
   unjustifiably mar Shakespeare's meter and music
14 did not stab
15 indeed, in fact
16 assisting
17 extent
18 (1) positions, ranks, titles, (2) reputations
19 dross ("money, cash": contemptuous)★
20 howl at
21 exasperate, snarl and bite at (like dogs "baiting" an animal)
22 practical experience
23 better suited/qualified
24 (1) restrictions, limitations, (2) behavior, morals
25 come now

Brutus   I say you are not.

Cassius   Urge me no more, I shall forget myself.   35

   Have mind upon[26] your health, tempt me no further.

Brutus   Away, slight[27] man!

Cassius   Is't possible?

Brutus   Hear me, for I will speak.

   Must I give way and room[28] to your rash choler?[29]

   Shall I be frighted when a madman stares?   40

Cassius   O ye gods, ye gods! Must I endure all this?

Brutus   All this? Ay, more. Fret[30] till your proud heart break.

   Go show your slaves how choleric you are,

   And make your bondmen tremble. Must I budge?[31]

   Must I observe[32] you? Must I stand and crouch[33]   45

   Under your testy[34] humor? By the gods,

   You shall digest[35] the venom of your spleen[36]

   Though it do split you. For, from this day forth,

   I'll use[37] you for my mirth, yea for my laughter,

   When you are waspish.

Cassius   Is[38] it come to this?   50

Brutus   You say you are a better soldier.

26 have mind upon = think/be careful of
27 (1) insignificant, (2) foolish
28 way and room = yield
29 anger
30 gnaw/torment/consume yourself
31 (1) flinch, wince, (2) move
32 pay attention to, follow
33 stoop
34 peevish, impatient, short-tempered
35 swallow, stomach
36 caprices, changeable/hot temper
37 deal with, treat
38 has

Let it appear so, make your vaunting[39] true,

And it shall please me well. For mine own part,

I shall be glad to learn of[40] noble men.

55 *Cassius* You wrong me every way. You wrong me, Brutus.

I said, an elder soldier, not a better.

Did I say "better"?

Brutus   If you did, I care not.

Cassius When Caesar lived, he durst not thus have moved me.

Brutus Peace, peace, you durst not so have tempted[41] him.

60 *Cassius* I durst not?

Brutus No.

Cassius What? Durst not tempt him?

Brutus   For your life you durst

not!

Cassius Do not presume too much upon my love,

I may do that I shall be sorry for.

65 *Brutus* You have done that[42] you should be sorry for.

There is no terror Cassius, in your threats,

For I am armed[43] so strong in honesty

That they pass by me as the idle wind,[44]

Which I respect not.[45] I did send to you

70 For certain sums of gold, which you denied[46] me,

For I can raise no money by vile means.

39 bragging, boasting

40 from

41 tested

42 the meter assists in understanding the emphasis, here: you HAVE done THAT you SHOULD be SORry FOR

43 armored

44 that THEY pass BY me AS the Idle WIND

45 respect not = pay no attention to

46 refused

By heaven, I had rather coin my heart,
And drop[47] my blood for drachmas, than to wring
From the hard hands of peasants their vile trash
By any indirection.[48] I did send   75
To you for gold to pay my legions,[49]
Which you denied me. Was that done like Cassius?
Should[50] I have answered Caius Cassius so?
When Marcus Brutus grows so covetous
To[51] lock such rascal counters[52] from his friends,   80
Be ready, gods, with all your thunderbolts,
Dash him to pieces!
Cassius   I denied you not.
Brutus You did.
Cassius I did not. He was but a fool that brought
My answer back. Brutus hath rived my heart.   85
A friend should bear his friend's infirmities,[53]
But Brutus makes mine greater than they are.
Brutus I do not, till you practice them on me.
Cassius You love me not.
Brutus   I do not like your faults.
Cassius A friendly eye could never see such faults.   90
Brutus A flatterer's would not, though they do appear
As huge as high Olympus.
Cassius Come, Antony, and young Octavius, come!

47 exude, spill
48 deviousness
49 infantry soldiers
50 would
51 as to
52 rascal counters = wretched/mean small/debased coins
53 weaknesses, frailties, flaws, defects

Cassius. Revenge yourselves alone[54] on Cassius,
95 For Cassius is a-weary of the world,
Hated by one he loves, braved[55] by his brother,
Checked[56] like a bondman, all his faults observed,
Set in a notebook, learned,[57] and conned by rote,[58]
To cast into my teeth. O I could weep
100 My spirit from[59] mine eyes! There is my dagger,
And here my naked breast. Within, a heart
Dearer than Plutus' mine,[60] richer[61] than gold.
If that thou beest[62] a Roman, take it forth.
I that denied thee gold will give my heart.
105 Strike as thou didst at Caesar. For I know
When thou didst hate him worst, thou lov'dst him better
Than ever thou lov'dst Cassius.

Brutus   Sheathe your dagger.
Be angry when you will, it shall have scope.[63]
Do what you will, dishonor shall be humor.
110 O Cassius, you are yoked with a lamb
That carries anger as the flint bears fire,
Who, much enforced, shows a hasty spark,
And straight is cold again.

Cassius   Hath Cassius lived

54 just, only
55 challenged
56 reviled, reproached, reprimanded
57 studied
58 conned by rote = memorized by repetition
59 out through
60 the gold and silver mines of Hades
61 worth more, of greater value
62 BEEist
63 have scope = enjoy free play / liberty ("achieve its purpose")

To be but mirth and laughter to his Brutus,

When grief, and blood ill-tempered, vexeth him?   115

Brutus   When I spoke that, I was ill-tempered too.

Cassius Do you confess so much? Give me your hand.

Brutus   And my heart too. 💚 ∈ love

Cassius   O Brutus!

Brutus   What's the matter?

Cassius Have not you love enough to bear with me,

When that rash humor which my mother gave me   120

Makes me forgetful?

Brutus   Yes Cassius, and from henceforth.

When you are over-earnest[64] with your Brutus,

He'll think your mother chides, and leave you so.[65]

Poet offstage (*within*) Let me go in to see the generals.

There is some grudge[66] between 'em, 'tis not meet   125

They be alone.

Lucilius   (*within*) You shall not come to them.

Poet   (*within*) Nothing but death shall ~~stay~~[67] me.
                       Stop

     ENTER POET, FOLLOWED BY LUCILIUS,
        TITINIUS, AND LUCIUS

Cassius How now? What's the matter?

Poet   For shame, you generals! What do you mean?

Love, and be friends, as two such men should be,   130

For I have seen more years I'm sure than ye.

Cassius Ha, ha! How vilely doth this cynic[68] rhyme!

---

64 over-earnest = over-impassioned, excessively emotional
65 leave you so = allow you to be thus/like that
66 discontent, ill-will
67 stop
68 Marcus Favonius was a philosopher of the cynic school (Diogenes et al.)

Brutus   Get you hence, sirrah. Saucy fellow, hence!

Cassius   Bear with him, Brutus, 'tis his fashion.

135 *Brutus*   I'll know his humor, when he knows his time.[69]

What should the wars do with these jigging[70] fools?

Companion,[71] hence!

Cassius   Away, away, be gone.

EXIT POET

Brutus   Lucilius and Titinius, bid the commanders

Prepare to lodge[72] their companies tonight.

140 *Cassius*   And come yourselves, and bring Messala with you

Immediately to us.

EXEUNT LUCILIUS AND TITINIUS

Brutus   Lucius, a bowl[73] of wine.

EXIT LUCIUS

Cassius   I did not think you could have been so angry.

Brutus   O Cassius, I am sick of[74] many griefs.

Cassius   Of your philosophy you make no use,

145   If you give place[75] to accidental evils.

Brutus   No man bears sorrow better. Portia is dead.

Cassius   Ha? Portia?

Brutus   She is dead.

69 his time = the proper time for him
70 rhyming and dancing
71 fellow
72 encamp, pitch camp
73 container
74 with/from
75 give place = yield

Cassius How 'scaped I killing when I crossed you so?

O insupportable and touching[76] loss! 150

Upon what sickness?

Brutus   Impatient of my absence,

And grief that young Octavius with Mark Antony

Have made themselves so strong. For with her death

That tidings came. With this she fell distract,[77]

And (her attendants absent) swallowed fire.[78] 155

Cassius And died so?

Brutus   Even so.

Cassius   O ye immortal gods!

ENTER LUCIUS, WITH WINE AND TAPERS

Brutus   Speak no more of her. Give me a bowl of wine.

In this I bury all unkindness, Cassius.

Cassius My heart is thirsty for that noble pledge.[79]

Fill, Lucius, till the wine o'erswell the cup. 160

I cannot drink too much of Brutus[80] love.

Brutus   Come in, Titinius!

EXIT LUCIUS

ENTER TITINIUS, WITH MESSALA

Welcome, good Messala.

Now sit we close[81] about this taper here,

76 pathetic
77 confused, deranged
78 she is said to have put hot coals in her mouth and choked to death
79 assurance of goodwill by drinking ("a toast")
80 modernization of Folio "Brutus" to "Brutus'" would mar Shakespeare's meter and music
81 in private

And call in question[82] our necessities.

Cassius Portia, art thou gone? *Portia's really dead?*

165 *Brutus*   No more, I pray you.

Messala, I have here receivèd letters, *Octavius? MarcAntony have power and are heading our way*

That young Octavius and Mark Antony

Come down upon us with a mighty power,

Bending[83] their expedition[84] toward Philippi.[85]

170 *Messala* Myself have letters of the selfsame tenor.[86]

Brutus With what addition?[87]

Messala That by proscription and bills of outlawry,

Octavius, Antony, and Lepidus

Have put to death an hundred senators.

175 *Brutus* Therein our letters do not well agree.

Mine speak of seventy senators that died

By their proscriptions, Cicero being one.

Cassius Cicero one!   *70 senators are dead*

Messala   Cicero is dead,

And by that order of proscription.

180   Had you your letters from your wife, my lord?

Brutus No, Messala.

Messala Nor nothing in your letters writ of her? *does he know yet Portia is dead*

Brutus Nothing, Messala.

Messala   That, methinks, is strange.

Brutus Why ask you? Hear you aught of her in yours?

185 *Messala* No, my lord. *have you heard anything*

82 call in question = examine
83 pointing, curving ("heading")
84 warlike enterprise
85 in Thrace, roughly 200 miles distant (FILliPEYE)
86 effect, substance
87 else (aDIseeOWN)

114

Brutus Now, as you are a Roman, tell me true.

Messala Then like a Roman bear the truth I tell,

For certain she is dead, and by strange manner.

Brutus Why farewell, Portia. We must die, Messala.

With meditating[88] that she must die once,   190

I have the patience to endure it now.

Messala Even[89] so great men great losses should[90] endure.

Cassius I have as much of this in art[91] as you,

But yet my nature could not bear it so.

Brutus Well, to our work alive.[92] What do you think   195

Of marching to Philippi presently?

Cassius I do not think it good.

Brutus   Your reason?

Cassius   This it is.

'Tis better that the enemy seek us,

So shall he waste his means, weary his soldiers,

Doing himself offense, whilst we lying still   200

Are full of rest, defense, and nimbleness.

Brutus Good reasons must, of force,[93] give place to better.

The people 'twixt Philippi and this ground[94]

Do stand but in a forced affection,[95]

For they have grudged us contribution.[96]   205

88 thinking, reflecting
89 just, exactly
90 ought to
91 (1) learning, philosophy, (2) skill (theatrics)
92 in the living state
93 necessity
94 this ground = here
95 goodwill (afFEKseeOWN)
96 (1) levies, payments, taxes, (2) aid, support

hus'll fight with them

The enemy, marching along by[97] them,

By them shall make a fuller number up,[98]

Come on refreshed, new-added, and encouraged.

From which advantage shall we cut him off,

210   If at Philippi we do face him there,

These people at our back.[99]

    Cassius   Hear me, good brother.

    Brutus Under your pardon.[100] You must note beside,

That we have tried[101] the utmost of[102] our friends.

Our legions are brim-full, our cause is ripe.

215   The enemy increaseth every day,

We at the height are ready to decline.

There is a tide in the affairs of men

Which, taken at the flood, leads on to fortune.

Omitted, all the voyage of their life

220   Is bound in shallows and in miseries.

On such a full sea are we now afloat,

And we must take the current when it serves,[103]

Or lose our ventures.[104]

Pastha

    Cassius—*he gave in*   Then, with your will, go on.

We'll along ourselves, and meet them at Philippi.

225   *Brutus* The deep of night is[105] crept upon our talk,

And nature[106] must obey necessity,

97 among
98 make a fuller number up = add to their forces
99 at our back = put behind us
100 under your pardon = with your leave/permission ("excuse me")
101 (1) tested, (2) extracted
102 from (if sense #2, just above)
103 assists, works
104 (1) fortunes, chances, (2) attempts, (3) adventures, enterprises
105 has
106 i.e., human nature

Which we will niggard[107] with a little rest.

There is no more to say?

Cassius   No more. Good night:

Early tomorrow will we rise, and hence.[108]

Brutus   Lucius.

ENTER LUCIUS

My gown.[109]

EXIT LUCIUS

Farewell, good Messala.   230

Good night, Titinius. Noble, noble Cassius,

Good night, and good repose.

Cassius   O my dear brother!

This was an ill beginning of the night.

Never[110] come such division[111] 'tween our souls!

Let it not, Brutus.

Brutus   Everything is well.

Cassius   Good night, my lord.

Brutus   Good night, good brother.

Titinius, Messala Good night, Lord Brutus.

Brutus   Farewell, every one.

EXEUNT ALL BUT BRUTUS

ENTER LUCIUS, WITH GOWN

107 put off ("cheat")
108 leave here
109 dressing gown (the word can also mean "nightgown," but as we learn, this garment has a pocket)
110 may there never
111 separation, disagreement, discord

117

Give me the gown. Where is thy instrument?

Lucius Here in the tent.

240 *Brutus*   What, thou speak'st drowsily?

Poor knave I blame thee not, thou art o'er-watched.[112]

Call Claudio and some other of my men,

I'll have them sleep on cushions in my tent.

Lucius Varro and Claudio!

ENTER VARRO AND CLAUDIO

245 *Varro* Calls my lord?

Brutus I pray you sirs, lie in my tent and sleep.

It may be I shall raise[113] you by and by

On business to my brother Cassius.

Varro So please you, we will stand and watch[114] your

pleasure.[115]

250 *Brutus* I will not have it so. Lie down, good sirs,

It may be I shall otherwise bethink me.

Look Lucius, here's the book I sought for so.

I put it in the pocket of my gown.

VARRO AND CLAUDIO LIE DOWN

Lucius I was sure your lordship did not give it me.

255 *Brutus* Bear with me, good boy, I am much forgetful.

Canst thou hold up thy heavy eyes awhile,

And touch[116] thy instrument a strain[117] or two?

112 fatigued from too much keeping himself awake
113 wake, rouse
114 be on the alert for
115 decision, discretion
116 strike/play on
117 melody, tune

Lucius Ay my lord, an't[118] please you.

Brutus   It does, my boy:

   I trouble thee too much, but thou art willing.

Lucius It is my duty, sir.   260

Brutus I should not urge thy duty past thy might,

   I know young bloods[119] look for[120] a time of rest.

Lucius I have slept, my lord, already.

Brutus It was well done,[121] and thou shalt sleep again.

   I will not hold thee long. If I do live,   265

   I will be good to thee.

LUCIUS PLAYS AND SINGS

   This is a sleepy tune. O murderous slumber,

   Lay'st thou thy leaden mace[122] upon my boy,

   That plays thee music? Gentle knave, good night.

   I will not do thee so much wrong to[123] wake thee.   270

   If thou dost nod,[124] thou break'st thy instrument.

   I'll take it from thee, and (good boy) good night.

   Let me see, let me see. Is not the leaf[125] turned down

   Where I left[126] reading? Here it is, I think.

ENTER CAESAR'S GHOST

   How ill this taper burns. Ha! Who comes here?   275

118 if it
119 (1) people, (2) bodies, (3) males, men
120 look for = (1) seek, (2) hope for
121 it was well done = good
122 club, staff
123 as to (fully)
124 drop your head when sleep suddenly descends
125 page
126 stopped

I think it is the weakness of mine eyes
That shapes[127] this monstrous apparition.
It comes upon[128] me. Art thou any thing?[129]
Art thou some god, some angel, or some devil,
280   That makest my blood cold and my hair to stare?[130]
Speak to me what thou art.

Ghost   Thy evil spirit, Brutus.

Brutus   Why comest thou?

Ghost   To tell thee thou shalt see me at Philippi.

Brutus   Well. Then I shall see thee again?

285 *Ghost*   Ay, at Philippi.

Brutus   Why I will see thee at Philippi then.

EXIT GHOST

Now[131] I have taken heart, thou vanishest.
Ill spirit, I would hold more talk with thee.
Boy – Lucius – Varro – Claudio – sirs! Awake! Claudio!
290 *Lucius*   The strings my lord are false.[132]
Brutus   He thinks he still is at his instrument.
Lucius, awake!

Lucius   My lord?

Brutus   Didst thou dream, Lucius, that[133] thou so criedst[134] out?

295 *Lucius*   My lord, I do not know that I did cry.

127 creates, forms
128 nearer / closer to
129 any thing = a palpable thing
130 stand on end
131 now that
132 out of tune
133 such, so that
134 called

Brutus	Yes, that thou didst. Didst thou see anything?
Lucius	Nothing, my lord.
Brutus	Sleep again, Lucius. Sirrah Claudio,

Fellow thou, awake!

Varro	My lord?
Claudio	My lord?
Brutus	Why did you so cry out, sirs, in your sleep?	300
Varro, Claudio	Did we, my lord?
Brutus	Ay. Saw you any thing?
Varro	No, my lord, I saw nothing.
Claudio	Nor I, my lord.
Brutus	Go and commend me to my brother Cassius.

Bid him set on his powers betimes before,

And we will follow.

Varro, Claudio	It shall be done, my lord.	305

EXEUNT

Act 5

SCENE I

Philippi

ENTER OCTAVIUS, ANTONY, AND SOLDIERS

Octavius Now Antony, our hopes are answerèd.
  You said the enemy would not come down,
  But keep the hills and upper regions.[1]
  It proves[2] not so. Their battles[3] are at hand,
5 They mean to warn[4] us at Philippi here,
  Answering before we do demand of them.
  Antony Tut, I am in their bosoms,[5] and I know
  Wherefore they do it. They could be content[6]
  To visit[7] other places, and come down[8]

[handwritten margin note: they mean to warn us at phillpi]

1 REEgeeOWNZ
2 is demonstrated to be
3 forces, armies
4 give us notice ("challenge")
5 hearts, secret thoughts
6 could be content = might be satisfied
7 attack
8 come down = sudden/surprising attack

With fearful bravery,[9] thinking by this face[10]
To fasten in our thoughts that they have courage.
But 'tis not so.

ENTER MESSENGER

Messenger   Prepare you, generals,
The enemy comes on in gallant show.
Their bloody sign[11] of battle is hung out,
And something to[12] be done immediately.   15
Antony   Octavius, lead your battle softly[13] on
Upon the left hand of the even field.
Octavius   Upon the right hand I, keep thou the left.
Antony   Why do you cross me in this exigent?[14]
Octavius   I do not cross you. But I will do so.[15]   20

DRUMS

ENTER FROM THE OTHER SIDE OF THE STAGE BRUTUS,
CASSIUS, LUCILIUS, TITINIUS, MESSALA, AND SOLDIERS

Brutus   They stand, and would[16] have parley.[17]
Cassius   Stand fast,[18] Titinius. We must out[19] and talk.
Octavius   Mark Antony, shall we give sign of battle?

9 fearful bravery = awesome defiance/bravado
10 (1) defiance, bold front, display, show, (2) thrust
11 signal, banner, flag (red in color, not literally "bloody")
12 must
13 (1) quietly, unobtrusively, (2) slowly
14 pressing/critical time, urgency, extremity
15 it my way ("thus")
16 wish to
17 a discussion
18 stay where you are ("as you were")
19 go out

Antony   No Caesar, we will answer on their charge.

25   Make forth, the generals[20] would have some words.

Octavius (_to a subordinate_) Stir not until the signal.

Brutus   Words before blows. Is it so,[21] countrymen?

Octavius Not that we love words better, as you do.

Brutus   Good words are better than bad strokes,[22] Octavius.

30   _Antony_   In your bad strokes, Brutus, you give good words.

        Witness the hole you made in Caesar's heart,

        Crying "Long live, hail, Caesar!"

Cassius   Antony,

        The posture[23] of your blows are yet unknown,

        But for[24] your words, they rob the Hybla[25] bees,

        And leave them honeyless.

35   _Antony_   Not stingless too.

Brutus   O yes, and soundless too.

        For you have stol'n their buzzing, Antony,

        And very wisely threat before you sting.

Antony   Villains. You did not so, when your vile daggers

40   Hacked one another[26] in the sides of Caesar.

        You showed your teeth[27] like apes, and fawned like hounds,

        And bowed like bondmen, kissing Caesar's feet,

        Whilst damnèd Casca, like a cur, behind[28]

20 i.e., the enemy generals
21 correct, right ("n'est-ce pas")
22 blows
23 military state
24 as for
25 town in Sicily, famous for its honey
26 hacked one another = cut/chopped one after the other
27 showed your teeth = grinned
28 (1) who had been standing back/toward the rear, held in reserve, (2) then, subsequently, (3) from the rear, at Caesar's back

Struck Caesar on the neck. O you flatterers!

Cassius Flatterers? Now Brutus, thank yourself. *(To Antony): Now you should think to us,*

This tongue had not offended so today, *I wanted to kill you*

If Cassius might have ruled.[29] *a long time ago* *If it were not for him, you would be dead.*

Octavius Come, come, the cause.[30] If arguing make us sweat,[31]

The proof of it will turn to redder drops.[32] Look,

I draw a sword against conspirators. 50

When think you that the sword goes up[33] again?

Never, till Caesar's three-and-thirty wounds

Be well avenged, or till another Caesar

Have added slaughter[34] to the sword of traitors.

Brutus Caesar, thou canst not die by traitors' hands, 55

Unless thou bring'st them with thee.

Octavius So I hope.

I was not born to die on Brutus' sword.

Brutus O if[35] thou wert the noblest of thy strain,[36] *the nicest*

Young man, thou couldst not die more honorable.

Cassius A peevish[37] schoolboy, worthless[38] of such honor, 60

Joined[39] with a masker and a reveler![40]

29 decided (i.e., had Antony been killed)
30 issue before us / real business
31 work hard, labor – thus producing "sweat"
32 the proof of it will turn to redder drops = that process will then produce blood
33 goes up = is sheathed
34 his own slaughter, if they kill him too
35 even if
36 ancestry, descent, lineage
37 (1) foolish, silly, (2) mischievous, malignant, quarrelsome, (3) headstrong, stubborn
38 unworthy
39 in league / allied with
40 a masker and a reveler = one who attends masquerades and leads a disorderly / merrymaking life

Antony Old[41] Cassius still! *still the same guy*

Octavius   Come Antony. Away!

Defiance, traitors, hurl we in your teeth.

If you dare fight today, come to the field.

65   If not, when[42] you have ~~stomachs~~.
                              guts

EXEUNT OCTAVIUS, ANTONY, AND THEIR SOLDIERS

Cassius Why now blow wind, swell billow, and swim bark![43]

The storm is up,[44] and all is on the hazard.

Brutus Ho Lucilius, hark, a word with you.

Lucilius (*stepping forward*) My lord?

BRUTUS AND LUCILIUS CONVERSE APART

70 *Cassius* Messala!

Messala (*stepping forward*) What says my general?

Cassius   Messala,

This is my birth day. As[45] this very day

Was Cassius born. Give me thy hand, Messala.

Be thou my witness that against my will   *on his birthday, he will*

75   (As Pompey was) am I compelled to set[46]   *bet all of their freedom*
                                              in this one battle,
Upon one battle all our liberties.   *against his will*

You know that I held Epicurus[47] strong,

And his opinion. Now I change my mind,

---

41 the same old

42 come whenever

43 boat (i.e., something smaller than what was called a "ship")

44 is up = has started

45 (1) just, even so, (2) at

46 (1) place, put, rest, (2) bet, wager

47 Greek philosopher, who did not believe in superstition or intervention by the gods (EpiKYUrus)

And partly credit[48] things that do presage.[49]

Coming from Sardis, on our former ensign[50]

Two mighty eagles fell,[51] and there they perched,

Gorging[52] and feeding from our soldiers' hands,

Who[53] to Philippi here consorted[54] us.

This morning are they fled away, and gone,

And in their steads do <u>ravens, crows, and kites</u>[55]

Fly o'er our heads, and downward look on us,

As[56] we were sickly[57] prey. Their shadows seem

A canopy[58] most fatal,[59] under which

Our army lies, ready to give up the ghost.

Messala Believe not so.

Cassius   I but believe it partly,   90

For I am fresh of spirit and resolved

To meet all perils very constantly.

Brutus (*rejoining Cassius*) Even so, Lucilius.

Cassius   Now, most noble

Brutus,

The[60] gods today stand friendly, that we may,

---

48 believe in, trust
49 foreshadow, predict, forecast (preSAGE)
50 former ensign = front/foremost/first banner/flag
51 dropped out of the sky
52 stuffing themselves
53 which eagles
54 accompanied, escorted, attended
55 hawks, falcons
56 as if
57 weak, feeble, unhealthy
58 overhanging covering (often used to mean "sky")
59 (1) prophetic, fateful, (2) ominous, doomed, deadly
60 let/may the

95   Lovers in peace, lead on[61] our days to age.[62]

But since the affairs of men rest still incertain,[63]

Let's reason with[64] the worst that may befall.

If we do lose this battle, then is this[65]

The very last time we shall speak together.

100   What are you then determinèd to do? *What are you going to do after this?*

   Brutus   Even[66] by the rule[67] of that philosophy

By which I did blame Cato[68] for the death

Which he did give himself. I know not how,

But I do find it cowardly and vile,

105   For fear of what might fall, so to prevent[69]

The time[70] of life. Arming[71] myself with patience

To stay[72] the providence[73] of some high powers

That govern us below.

   Cassius   Then, if we lose this battle,

You are contented to be led in triumph *are you ok with being led through Rome as a prisoner*

110   Thorough the streets of Rome?

   Brutus   No, Cassius, no. Think not, thou noble Roman,

That ever Brutus will go bound to Rome.

Never.

---

61 lead on = advance

62 old age

63 still incertain = always uncertain

64 reason with = discuss, think about

65 is this = this is

66 exactly, precisely

67 principles, regulations, maxims

68 Portia's father, who committed suicide, thinking he would be killed

69 anticipate

70 duration, length (here, meaning the "end" of his life)

71 I am arming

72 wait for

73 wise arrangements / governance

He bears too great[74] a mind. But this same day

Must end that work the[75] Ides of March begun,

And whether we shall meet again I know not. 115

Therefore our everlasting farewell take.

For ever, and for ever, farewell, Cassius.

If we do meet again, why we shall smile.

If not, why then this parting was well made.

Cassius For ever, and for ever, farewell Brutus! 120

If we do meet again, we'll smile indeed.

If not, 'tis true this parting was well made.

Brutus Why then lead on. O that a man might know

The end of this day's business ere it come.

But it sufficeth that the day will end, 125

And then the end is known. Come ho, away!

EXEUNT

74 courageous
75 which the

SCENE 2

Philippi, the battlefield

ALARUM[1]

ENTER BRUTUS AND MESSALA

Brutus Ride, ride, Messala, ride, and give these bills[2]
Unto the legions on the other side.

LOUD ALARUM

Let them set on at once. For I perceive
But cold demeanor[3] in Octavius' wing,[4]
5 And sudden push gives them the overthrow.
Ride, ride, Messala, let them all come down.

EXEUNT

1 call to arms
2 documents
3 cold demeanor = dispirited/weak behavior
4 the flank/side of the army

SCENE 3

Another part of the battlefield

ALARUMS

ENTER CASSIUS AND TITINIUS

Cassius   O look Titinius, look, the villains[1] fly!
  Myself have to mine own turned enemy.
  This ensign[2] here of mine was turning back.
  I slew the coward, and did take it from him.
Titinius   O Cassius, Brutus gave the word too early,   5
  Who having some advantage on Octavius,
  Took it too eagerly. His soldiers fell to spoil,
  Whilst we by Antony are all enclosed.

ENTER PINDARUS

Pindarus   Fly further off, my lord. Fly further off,
  Mark Antony is in your tents, my lord.   10
  Fly therefore, noble Cassius, fly far off.
Cassius   This hill is far enough. Look, look, Titinius.
  Are those my tents where I perceive the fire?
Titinius   They are, my lord.
Cassius   Titinius, if thou lovest me,
  Mount thou my horse, and hide[3] thy spurs in him,   15
  Till he have brought thee up to yonder troops,
  And here again, that I may rest assured
  Whether yond troops are friend or enemy.

---

1 i.e., his own soldiers, villainous for being cowards
2 i.e., the soldier carrying the banner/flag
3 i.e., dig the spurs all the way in

Titinius I will be here again, even with a thought.[4]

Find out if those [struck: little] troops are ours or enemy's

EXIT TITINIUS

20 *Cassius* Go Pindarus, get higher on that hill,

go on a hill and watch Titinius

My sight was ever thick.[5] Regard Titinius,

And tell me what thou notest about the field.

PINDARUS ASCENDS THE HILL

This day I breathèd first, time is come round,

And where I did begin, there shall I end,

My life is at it's end

25 My life is run his compass.[6] Sirrah, what news?

Pindarus (*above*) O my lord!

Cassius What news?

Pindarus (*above*) Titinius is enclosèd round about

With horsemen, that make to[7] him on the spur,

30 Yet he spurs on. Now they are almost on him.

Now, Titinius! Now some light.[8] O he lights too.

He's ta'en. *he fallen by the horses*

The triumphered him

SHOUT

And hark, they shout for joy.

Cassius Come down, behold no more.

O coward that I am, to live so long,

35 To see my best friend ta'en before my face!

he sent Titinius to his death

Titinius PINDARUS DESCENDS

4 even with = as quick as a thought

5 dense, dull

6 is run his compass = has run its measure/circle

7 make to = come toward

8 some light = some of the attackers dismount

Come hither, sirrah.
In Parthia did I take thee prisoner,
And then I swore thee,[9] saving of [10] thy life,
That whatsoever I did bid thee do
Thou shouldst attempt it. Come now, keep thine oath,   40
Now be a freeman,[11] and with this good sword
That ran through Caesar's bowels, search[12] this bosom.
Stand[13] not to answer. Here, take thou the hilts,[14]
And when my face is covered, as 'tis now,
Guide thou the sword.

PINDARUS STABS HIM

Caesar, thou art revenged,   45
Even with the sword that killed thee.

CASSIUS DIES

Pindarus So[15] I am free, yet would not so have been,
Durst I have done my will.[16] O Cassius,
Far from this country Pindarus shall run,
Where never Roman shall take note of him.   50

EXIT PINDARUS

ENTER TITINIUS AND MESSALA

9 swore thee = made you swear
10 saving of = except for
11 be a freeman = I here by set you free (many slaves were wartime captives)
12 investigate, probe
13 delay, wait
14 i.e., cross-barred hilts were necessary for heavier swords
15 thus
16 i.e., he could not disobey Cassius and break his oath, but he did not wish to
   kill him

133

Titinus wasn't captured. They were his enemies

Messala It is but change,[17] Titinius. For Octavius

Is overthrown by noble Brutus' power,

As Cassius' legions are by Antony.

Titinius These tidings will well comfort Cassius.

Messala Where did you leave him?

55 *Titinius*   All disconsolate,

With Pindarus his bondman, on this hill.

Messala Is not that he that lies upon the ground?

Titinius He lies not like the living. O my heart!

Messala Is not that he?

Titinius   No, this was he, Messala,

60 But Cassius is no more. O setting sun,

As in thy red rays thou dost sink tonight,

So in his red blood Cassius' day is set. *none to Titinius*

Cassius is the sun of Rome The sun of Rome is set. Our day is gone,

Clouds, dews,[18] and dangers come, our deeds are done!

65 Mistrust[19] of my success[20] hath done this deed.

Messala Mistrust of good success hath done this deed.[21]

O hateful error, melancholy's child.

Why dost thou show to the apt thoughts of men

The things that are not? O error soon[22] conceived,

70 Thou never comest unto a happy birth,

But kill'st the mother that engendered[23] thee.

Titinius What, Pindarus? Where art thou, Pindarus?

17 an exchange

18 dampness (then considered dangerous for men's health)

19 doubt

20 result, fortune (i.e., that he had identified the unknown troops as friends)

21 (the repetition is spoken slowly, somberly)

22 quickly, immediately

23 conceived

Messala Seek him, Titinius, whilst I go to meet
  The noble Brutus, thrusting[24] this report
  Into his ears. I may say, thrusting it, 75
  For piercing steel and darts envenomed
  Shall be as welcome to the ears of Brutus
  As tidings of this sight.
Titinius   Hie you, Messala,
  And I will seek for Pindarus the while.

EXIT MESSALA

  Why didst thou send me forth, brave Cassius? 80
  Did I not meet thy friends, and did not they
  Put on my brows this wreath of victory,
  And bid me give it thee? Didst thou not hear their shouts?
  Alas, thou hast misconstrued everything!
  But hold[25] thee, take this garland on thy brow. 85
  Thy Brutus bid me give it thee, and I
  Will do his bidding. Brutus, come apace,[26]
  And see how I regarded[27] Caius Cassius.
  By your leave, gods. This is a Roman's part.
  Come, Cassius' sword, and find Titinius' heart. 90

TITINIUS KILLS HIMSELF

ALARUM

ENTER MESSALA, WITH BRUTUS, CATO, STRATO,
VOLUMNIUS, AND LUCILIUS

24 forcing, striking, piercing
25 wait
26 quickly
27 (1) took care of, (2) valued, esteemed, considered

135

Brutus   Where, where, Messala, doth his body lie?

Messala   Lo, yonder, and Titinius mourning it.

Brutus   Titinius' face is upward.

Cato   He is slain.

Brutus   O Julius Caesar, thou art mighty yet,

95   Thy spirit walks abroad and turns our swords

In our own proper[28] entrails.

LOW ALARUMS

Cato   Brave Titinius,

Look whe'er[29] he have not crowned dead Cassius.

Brutus   Are yet two Romans living such as these?

The last of all the Romans, fare thee well!

100   It is impossible that ever Rome

Should breed thy fellow.[30] Friends, I owe more tears

To this dead man than you shall see me pay.

I shall find time, Cassius. I shall find time.

Come therefore, and to Tharsus send his body.

105   His funerals shall[31] not be in our camp,

Lest it discomfort us. Lucilius come,

And come young Cato, let us to the field.

Labio and Flavio,[32] set our battles on.

'Tis three o'clock, and Romans, yet ere night,

110   We shall try fortune in a second fight.

EXEUNT

28 own proper = own
29 whether
30 match, counterpart
31 must
32 names drawn from Shakespeare's sources; these characters neither speak nor
    are elsewhere mentioned in the play

SCENE 4

Another part of the battlefield

ALARUM

ENTER SOLDIERS OF BOTH ARMIES, FIGHTING, THEN BRUTUS,
CATO, LUCILIUS, AND OTHERS

Brutus   Yet, countrymen, O yet hold up your heads!

Cato   What bastard[1] doth not? Who will go with me?

I will proclaim my name about the field.

I am the son of Marcus Cato, ho,

A foe to tyrants, and my country's friend.   5

I am the son of Marcus Cato, ho!

SOLDIERS ENTER, AND FIGHT

Lucilius   And I am Brutus, Marcus Brutus, I,

Brutus, my country's friend. Know me for[2] Brutus!

CATO IS KILLED

O young and noble Cato, art thou down?

Why now thou diest as bravely as Titinius,   10

And mayst be honored, being Cato's son.

First Soldier Yield, or thou diest.

Lucilius   Only I yield[3] to die.

There is so much,[4] that thou wilt kill me straight.

Kill Brutus, and be honored in his death.

---

1 i.e., someone not a true/legitimate Roman

2 as (to signal to/remind the audience that Lucilius is only pretending to be Brutus?)

3 only I yield = I yield only

4 so much = to be gained

15 *First Soldier* We must not. A noble prisoner.

Second Soldier Room ho!⁵ Tell Antony, Brutus is ta'en.

First Soldier I'll tell the news. Here comes the general.

ENTER ANTONY

Brutus is ta'en, Brutus is ta'en, my lord.

Antony Where is he?

20 *Lucilius* Safe, Antony, Brutus is safe enough.

I dare assure thee that no enemy

Shall ever take alive the noble Brutus.

The gods defend him from so great a shame!

When you do find him, or⁶ alive or dead,

25 He will be found like Brutus, like himself.

Antony This is not Brutus, friend, but I assure you,

A prize no less in worth. Keep this man safe,

Give him all kindness. I had rather have

Such men my friends than enemies. Go on,

30 And see whether Brutus be alive or dead,

And bring us word unto Octavius' tent

How everything is chanced.

EXEUNT

5 out of the way!
6 either/whether

SCENE 5

Another part of the battlefield

ENTER BRUTUS, DARDANIUS, CLITUS,
STRATO, AND VOLUMNIUS

Brutus	Come, poor remains of friends, rest on this rock.
Clitus	Statilius showed the torchlight,[1] but my lord,
	He came not back. He is or[2] ta'en or slain.
Brutus	Sit thee down, Clitus. Slaying is the word,
	It is a deed in fashion.[3] Hark thee, Clitus.

BRUTUS WHISPERS TO CLITUS

Clitus	What I, my lord? No, not for all the world.
Brutus	Peace then, no words.
Clitus	I'll rather kill myself.
Brutus	Hark thee, Dardanius.

BRUTUS WHISPERS TO DARDANIUS

Dardanius	Shall I do such a deed?
Clitus	O Dardanius.
Dardanius	O Clitus.
Clitus	What ill request did Brutus make to thee?
Dardanius	To kill him, Clitus. Look, he meditates.
Clitus	Now is that noble vessel[4] full[5] of grief
	That it runs over even[6] at his eyes.

5

10

---

1 i.e., as a signal of the success of a reconnaissance mission
2 either
3 current use / style / custom
4 man (figurative)
5 so full
6 steadily, constantly

Brutus   Come hither, good Volumnius,[7] list a word.

Volumnius What says my lord?

15 *Brutus*   Why, this, Volumnius.

The ghost of Caesar hath appeared to me

Two several times by night. At Sardis, once,

And this last night, here in Philippi fields.

I know my hour is come.

Volumnius   Not so, my lord.

20 *Brutus*   Nay, I am sure it is, Volumnius.

Thou seest the world, Volumnius, how it goes.

Our enemies have beat us to the pit.[8]

LOW ALARUMS

It is more worthy to leap in ourselves,

Than tarry till they push us. Good Volumnius,

25 Thou know'st that we two went to school together.

Even[9] for that our love of old, I prithee

Hold thou my sword–hilts, whilst I run on it.

Volumnius That's not an office[10] for a friend, my lord.

CONTINUING ALARUM

Clitus   Fly, fly, my lord, there is no tarrying here.

30 *Brutus*   Farewell to you, and you, and you, Volumnius.

Strato, thou hast been all this while asleep.

Farewell to thee too, Strato. Countrymen,

My heart doth joy that yet in all my life

7 vaLOOMneeUS
8 beat us to the pit = trapped/snared/driven us into the pit
9 exactly, precisely
10 duty ("job")

140

I found no man but he was true to me.
I shall have glory by this losing day   35
More than Octavius, and Mark Antony,
By this vile conquest shall attain unto.
So fare you well at once,[11] for Brutus' tongue
Hath almost ended his life's history:
Night hangs upon mine eyes, my bones would[12] rest,   40
That have but[13] labored to attain this hour.

ALARUM

CRY WITHIN, "FLY, FLY, FLY!"

Clitus   Fly, my lord, fly.
Brutus   Hence. I will follow.

EXEUNT CLITUS, DARDANIUS, AND VOLUMNIUS

I prithee, Strato, stay thou by thy lord.
Thou art a fellow of a good respect.[14]
Thy life hath had some smatch[15] of honor in it.   45
Hold then my sword, and turn away thy face,
While I do run upon it. Wilt thou, Strato?
Strato   Give me your hand first. Fare you well, my lord.
Brutus   Farewell, good Strato.

BRUTUS RUNS ON HIS SWORD

Caesar, now be still.

11 at once = once and for all
12 wish to
13 only
14 standing, esteem
15 indication, taste, flavor

[handwritten: still feels guilty]

50   I killed not thee with half so good a will.

[handwritten: he's putting Caesar's ghost to rest]

BRUTUS DIES

ALARUM

RETREAT[16]

ENTER OCTAVIUS, ANTONY, MESSALA,
LUCILIUS, AND SOLDIERS

Octavius   What man is that?

Messala   My master's man. Strato, where is thy master?

Strato   Free from the bondage you are in, Messala,

The conquerors can but make a fire of him.

55   For Brutus only overcame himself,

And no man else hath honor by his death.

Lucilius   So Brutus should[17] be found. I thank thee, Brutus,

That thou hast proved Lucilius[18] saying true.

Octavius   All that served Brutus, I will entertain[19] them.

60   Fellow, wilt thou bestow thy time with me?

Strato   Ay, if Messala will prefer[20] me to you.

Octavius   Do so, good Messala.

Messala   How died my master, Strato?

Strato   I held the sword, and he did run on it.   *[handwritten: he committed ritual suicide]*

65 *Messala*   Octavius, then take him to follow thee,

That[21] did the latest[22] service to my master.

---

16 signal to call off pursuit
17 ought to
18 "Lucilius's" would be a prosodic monstrosity, even though modern usage
   prefers it
19 retain, keep
20 recommend
21 he who
22 last

Antony   This was the noblest Roman of them all.

All the conspirators save only he

Did that[23] they did in envy of great Caesar.

He only, in[24] a general honest thought,   70

And common good to all, made[25] one of them.

His life was gentle, and the elements[26]

So mixed in him that Nature might stand up

And say to all the world, "This was a man."

Octavius   According to his virtue let us use[27] him

With all respect and rites of burial.

Within my tent his bones tonight shall lie,

Most like a soldier ordered[28] honorably.

So call the field to rest,[29] and let's away,

To part[30] the glories of this happy day.   80

EXEUNT

23 that which
24 from
25 made himself
26 constituent portions, various components
27 treat
28 prepared
29 call the field to rest = summon (via trumpet calls) the fighting to desist/
  break off
30 share

143

*T*he *Tragedy of Julius Caesar* is a very satisfying play, as a play, and is universally regarded as a work of considerable aesthetic dignity. We tend to read it first when we are in school, because it is so clear and simple a drama that our teachers find it suitable for us there. I have seen it only once on stage, once on television, and once as a film, and found none of these three presentations quite adequate, the problem in each case being with the actor who misplayed Brutus. Directors and actors seem to place more of Hamlet in Brutus than Shakespeare himself set there, and Brutus just cannot sustain Hamlet's aura. Hamlet scarcely can speak without extending our consciousness into the farthest ranges, but there is a narcissistic, rather spoiled quality to the perhaps excessively noble Brutus, and he does not achieve ghostlier demarcations, keener sounds, until his fortunes begin to fail.

Modern critics find somewhat problematical Shakespeare's supposed political stance in *Julius Caesar.* Presumably Shakespeare, as an Elizabethan royalist, is unhappy about the assassination of Caesar, and yet Brutus is the tragic hero. Caesar is in decay, a touch vainglorious, the conqueror dwindled into a ruler who accepts flattery. But however the politics of *Julius Caesar* are to be resolved, the play seems problematical in most respects. Its characters, including even Brutus, are not endless to meditation, and its rhetoric does not reverberate so as to suggest a beyond. There is no Marlovian element in *Julius Caesar*, no hero-villains of Hermetic ambition or Machiavellian intensity, no surpassingly eloquent and outrageous overreachers. Whether from North's Plutarch or from Seneca, or more likely from a strain in his own nature, Shakespeare brings forth a Stoic music with its own dying falls, but without a grudge or bias against our given condition. Brutus essentially is a Stoic, acutely self-conscious and self-regarding, with a touch of Virgil's Aeneas in him. But he has been too much admired in Rome, and he greatly admires himself. A. D. Nuttall is useful in contrasting Brutus and his Stoicism to Antony's affective opportunism: "Brutus, the aristocrat, his theoretic Stoicism borne on a foundation of shame-culture, on ancient heroic dignity, belongs to the Roman past. He can do the Stoic trick (rather like 'isolating' a muscle) of separating his reason from his passions but he cannot exploit his own motivating passions with the coolness of an Antony. With all his fondness for statuesque postures Brutus remains morally more spontaneous than Antony."

Where is Cassius on this scale of moral spontaneity? He plays upon Brutus in order to bring him into the conspiracy, but then yields to Brutus both as to Antony's survival and on granting Antony permission to speak at Caesar's funeral. When he yields a third time and consents, against his will, to stake everything upon battle at Philippi, he completes the irony of this own undoing, and Caesar's ghost is avenged. The irony could be interpreted as a dialectic of conscience and affection, since Cassius politically seduced Brutus by exploiting the Stoic hero's moral spontaneity.

Cassius is destroyed by Brutus' incompetent political and military decisions, to which Cassius yields out of affection, but also because he must accept the only role possible for Brutus in any enterprise.

Cassius is the one figure in the play who might have benefited by a touch of Marlovian force or antithetical intensity, but Shakespeare preferred to maintain his own Stoic control in representing a Stoic tragedy. We ought to marvel that Shakespeare, a year or so later, could venture upon the infinite by writing *Hamlet,* where every current is antithetical and far beyond merely rational controls. *Julius Caesar* has more in common with *Henry V* than with *Hamlet,* just as the two parts of *Henry IV* reach out to *As You Like It* and *Hamlet.* What is excluded from *Julius Caesar* is the madness of great wit, the exuberance of Falstaff, of Rosalind, and of one of the endless aspects of Hamlet. As we miss Falstaff in *Henry V,* so we miss someone, anyone, who could cause *Julius Caesar* to flare up for us. Shakespeare, with a curiously Stoic forbearance, subdued himself to his subject, though we do not know why.

The results of this uncharacteristic *ascesis* are surely mixed. We receive clarity and nobility, and lose nearly everything that makes Shakespeare unique. Dr. Samuel Johnson's summary speaks to this better than I can: "Of this tragedy many particular passages deserve regard, and the contention and reconcilement of Brutus and Cassius is universally celebrated; but I have never been strongly agitated in perusing it, and think it somewhat cold and unaffecting, comparing with some other of Shakespeare's plays; his adherence to the real story, and to Roman manners, seems to have impeded the natural vigour of his genius."

Whatever the impediments, *Julius Caesar* is an anomaly among Shakespeare's mature plays in that it possesses his originality in language, to a fair degree, yet is almost wholly devoid of his principal originality in representation. Not even Brutus changes by listening to himself ruminate. How much difference can we hear between Brutus at the beginning of act 2 and Brutus near to the end of act 5? Brooding upon the probable change in a crowned Caesar, Brutus takes the responsibility of prophesying the change: "It is the bright day that brings forth the adder, / And that craves wary walking" (2.1.14–15).

Poor Brutus, once embarked upon his venture, never encounters his own bright day. Shakespeare subtly allows the Stoic hero a continuous nobility down to the end, while also allowing Brutus to be deaf to the irony of his own final self-praise: "Countrymen, / My heart doth joy that yet in all my life / I found no man but he was true to me" (5.5.32–34).

We wince, however sympathetic we find Brutus, since he seems to have forgotten Caesar's last words, with their shock that Brutus, of all men, should have been untrue to his friend Caesar. Brutus'"As Caesar lov'd me, I weep for him" (3.2.23–24) does not linger in us, but we do remember Antony's bitter eloquence: "For Brutus, as you know, was Caesar's angel" (3.2.176).

Perhaps Shakespeare's politics did inhibit his profoundest powers in *Julius Caesar.* The tragedy of Brutus and the crime against the monarch could not be reconciled with one another, and Shakespeare, divided against himself, found he could not be wholly true to Brutus.

Instead, he intimated a remarkably indirect complexity in the Caesar-Brutus relationship. His prime source, Sir Thomas North's Plutarch, told him that much of Rome believed Brutus to be Caesar's natural son. Read very closely, the play hints at a tragedy of patricide, in which Brutus does not allow himself to confront the possibility that he is a Caesar and not a Brutus. His pride that he is descended from the family that expelled the tyrant Tarquin from Rome, thus saving the Republic, is rendered uneasy by what he will not mention even to himself, that he may well be Caesar's bastard. But why did Shakespeare cover this over, and can it be read between the lines? I cannot revisit the play without encountering this ambiguity that secretly spurs Brutus' ambivalence.

This ambivalence is subtly oedipal, as is Macbeth's pathos in regard to Duncan. Like father, like son: Caesar and Brutus share an incapacity to change. The hidden father and the apparent son possess also in common a fatal egocentricity: each is given to referring to himself in the third person. Again, Caesar and Brutus manifest a peculiar blindness in regard to the motivations of other men. Both merge Rome into themselves, rather than themselves into Rome.

When Brutus tells the people: "As Caesar loved me, I weep for him," where is his love for Caesar, whom (by some reports) he stabbed in the genitals? Many in Shakespeare's audience had North's Plutarch in their consciousness, and thus knew that Suetonius repeated the Roman gossip of Brutus having been Caesar's bastard. Why did Shakespeare evade this very dramatic possibility? So wary is Shakespeare, that he portrays only one encounter between Caesar and Brutus before the scene of murder. The meeting, in which putative father and assassin-son briefly are alone together, is blatantly commonplace. Caesar asks the time, Brutus says it is 8:00 A.M., and Caesar gravely thanks his son "for your pains and courtesy (2.2.115)."

Shakespeare, richest of all writers, is also the most elliptical. We never confront Antony and Cleopatra in a domestic context: What are they occupied with, besides sex and politics, when they are alone together? Why do Edmund and Lear never speak to one another? Do Othello and Desdemona ever consummate their marriage? Are both Othello and Iago impotent? Shakespeare wants us to solve these matters for ourselves.

Mark Antony tells the Romans that Brutus was "Caesar's angel," meaning Caesar's genius as well as his favorite. Gossip would have told the crowd what Shakespeare will not tell us, though he allows Cassius to hint at it. Whether Shakespeare was politically nervous, since the pope already had excommunicated Queen Elizabeth, we just do not know. I suspect that the elliptical was one of Shakespeare's favorite modes and that he delighted in leaving things out. Brutus says that we all stand up against the spirit of Caesar and that in the spirit of man there is no blood. But Caesar and Brutus are fated to be one another's evil spirits, and I suggest that their mutual tragedy is their common blood.

FURTHER READING

This is not a bibliography but a selective set of starting places.

Texts

Shakespeare, William. *The First Folio of Shakespeare,* 2d ed. Edited by
Charlton Hinman. Introduction by Peter W. M. Blayney. New York:
W. W. Norton, 1996.

————. *The Tragedie of Julius Caesar: New Variorum Edition.* Edited by
Horace Howard Furness, Jr. Philadelphia: Lippincott, 1913.

Language

Dobson, E. J. *English Pronunciation, 1500–1700.* 2d ed. Oxford: Oxford
University Press, 1968.

Houston, John Porter. *The Rhetoric of Poetry in the Renaissance and
Seventeenth Century.* Baton Rouge: Louisiana State University Press,
1983.

————. *Shakespearean Sentences: A Study in Style and Syntax.* Baton
Rouge: Louisiana State University Press, 1988.

Kermode, Frank. *Shakespeare's Language.* New York: Farrar, Straus and
Giroux, 2000.

Kökeritz, Helge. *Shakespeare's Pronunciation.* New Haven: Yale
University Press, 1953.

Lanham, Richard A. *The Motives of Eloquence: Literary Rhetoric in the
Renaissance.* New Haven and London: Yale University Press, 1976.

The Oxford English Dictionary: Second Edition on CD-ROM, version 3.0.
    New York: Oxford University Press, 2002.

Raffel, Burton. *From Stress to Stress: An Autobiography of English Prosody.*
    Hamden, Conn.: Archon Books, 1992.

Ronberg, Gert. *A Way with Words: The Language of English Renaissance
    Literature.* London: Arnold, 1992.

Trousdale, Marion. *Shakespeare and the Rhetoricians.* Chapel Hill:
    University of North Carolina Press, 1982.

Culture

Bindoff, S. T. *Tudor England.* Baltimore: Penguin, 1950.

Bradbrook, M. C. *Shakespeare: The Poet in His World.* New York:
    Columbia University Press, 1978.

Brown, Cedric C., ed. *Patronage, Politics, and Literary Tradition in England,
    1558–1658.* Detroit, Mich.: Wayne State University Press, 1993.

Bush, Douglas. *Prefaces to Renaissance Literature.* New York: W. W.
    Norton, 1965.

Buxton, John. *Elizabethan Taste.* London: Harvester, 1963.

Cowan, Alexander. *Urban Europe, 1500–1700.* New York: Oxford
    University Press, 1998.

Driver, Tom E. *The Sense of History in Greek and Shakespearean Drama.*
    New York: Columbia University Press, 1960.

Finucci, Valeria, and Regina Schwartz, eds. *Desire in the Renaissance:
    Psychoanalysis and Literature.* Princeton, N.J.: Princeton University
    Press, 1994.

Fumerton, Patricia, and Simon Hunt, eds. *Renaissance Culture and the
    Everyday.* Philadelphia: University of Pennsylvania Press, 1999.

Halliday, F. E. *Shakespeare in His Age.* South Brunswick, N.J.: Yoseloff,
    1965.

Harrison, G. B., ed. *The Elizabethan Journals: Being a Record of Those
    Things Most Talked of During the Years 1591–1597.* Abridged ed. 2 vols.
    New York: Doubleday Anchor, 1965.

Harrison, William. *The Description of England: The Classic Contemporary
    [1577] Account of Tudor Social Life.* Edited by Georges Edelen.

Washington, D.C.: Folger Shakespeare Library, 1968. Reprint, New York: Dover, 1994.

Jardine, Lisa. "Introduction." In Jardine, *Reading Shakespeare Historically.* London: Routledge, 1996.

————. *Worldly Goods: A New History of the Renaissance.* London: Macmillan, 1996.

Jeanneret, Michel. *A Feast of Words: Banquets and Table Talk in the Renaissance.* Translated by Jeremy Whiteley and Emma Hughes. Chicago: University of Chicago Press, 1991.

Kernan, Alvin. *Shakespeare, the King's Playwright: Theater in the Stuart Court, 1603–1613.* New Haven: Yale University Press, 1995.

Lockyer, Roger. *Tudor and Stuart Britain, 1471–1714.* London: Longmans, 1964.

Norwich, John Julius. *Shakespeare's Kings: The Great Plays and the History of England in the Middle Ages, 1337–1485.* New York: Scribner, 2000.

Rose, Mary Beth, ed. *Renaissance Drama as Cultural History: Essays from Renaissance Drama, 1977–1987.* Evanston, Ill.: Northwestern University Press, 1990.

Schmidgall, Gary. *Shakespeare and the Courtly Aesthetic.* Berkeley: University of California Press, 1981.

Smith, G. Gregory, ed. *Elizabethan Critical Essays.* 2 vols. Oxford: Clarendon Press, 1904.

Tillyard, E. M. W. *The Elizabethan World Picture.* London: Chatto and Windus, 1943. Reprint, Harmondsworth: Penguin, 1963.

Willey, Basil. *The Seventeenth Century Background: Studies in the Thought of the Age in Relation to Poetry and Religion.* New York: Columbia University Press, 1933. Reprint, New York: Doubleday, 1955.

Wilson, F. P. *The Plague in Shakespeare's London.* 2d ed. Oxford: Oxford University Press, 1963.

Wilson, John Dover. *Life in Shakespeare's England: A Book of Elizabethan Prose.* 2d ed. Cambridge: Cambridge University Press, 1913. Reprint, Harmondsworth: Penguin, 1944.

Zimmerman, Susan, and Ronald F. E. Weissman, eds. *Urban Life in the Renaissance.* Newark: University of Delaware Press, 1989.

Dramatic Development

Cohen, Walter. *Drama of a Nation: Public Theater in Renaissance England and Spain.* Ithaca, N.Y.: Cornell University Press, 1985.

Dessen, Alan C. *Shakespeare and the Late Moral Plays.* Lincoln: University of Nebraska Press, 1986.

Fraser, Russell A., and Norman Rabkin, eds. *Drama of the English Renaissance.* 2 vols. Upper Saddle River, N.J.: Prentice Hall, 1976.

Happé, Peter, ed. *Tudor Interludes.* Harmondsworth: Penguin, 1972.

Laroque, François. *Shakespeare's Festive World: Elizabethan Seasonal Entertainment and the Professional Stage.* Translated by Janet Lloyd. Cambridge: Cambridge University Press, 1991.

Norland, Howard B. *Drama in Early Tudor Britain, 1485–1558.* Lincoln: University of Nebraska Press, 1995.

Theater and Stage

Doran, Madeleine. *Endeavors of Art: A Study of Form in Elizabethan Drama.* Milwaukee: University of Wisconsin Press, 1954.

Gibson, Leslie Joy. *Squeaking Cleopatras: The Elizabethan Boy Player.* Stroud, U.K.: Sutton, 2000.

Grene, David. *The Actor in History: Studies in Shakespearean Stage Poetry.* University Park: Pennsylvania State University Press, 1988.

Gurr, Andrew. *Playgoing in Shakespeare's London.* Cambridge: Cambridge University Press, 1987.

———. *The Shakespearian Stage, 1574–1642.* 3d ed. Cambridge: Cambridge University Press, 1992.

Halliday, F. E. *A Shakespeare Companion, 1564–1964.* Rev. ed. Harmondsworth: Penguin, 1964.

Harrison, G. B. *Elizabethan Plays and Players.* Ann Arbor: University of Michigan Press, 1956.

Holmes, Martin. *Shakespeare and His Players.* New York: Scribner, 1972.

Ingram, William. *The Business of Playing: The Beginnings of the Adult Professional Theater in Elizabethan London.* Ithaca, N.Y.: Cornell University Press, 1992.

Kastan, David Scott. *Shakespeare and the Book.* Cambridge: Cambridge University Press, 2001.

LeWinter, Oswald, ed. *Shakespeare in Europe.* Cleveland, Ohio: Meridian, 1963.

Marcus, Leah S. *Unediting the Renaissance: Shakespeare, Marlowe, Milton.* London: Routledge, 1996.

Orgel, Stephen. *The Authentic Shakespeare, and Other Problems of the Early Modern Stage.* New York: Routledge, 2002.

Ornstein, Robert. *A Kingdom for a Stage: The Achievement of Shakespeare's History Plays.* Cambridge, Mass: Harvard University Press, 1972.

———. *Shakespeare's Comedies: From Roman Farce to Romantic Mystery.* Newark: University of Delaware Press, 1986.

Salgado, Gamini. *Eyewitnesses of Shakespeare: First Hand Accounts of Performances, 1590–1890.* New York: Barnes and Noble, 1975.

Stern, Tiffany. *Rehearsal from Shakespeare to Sheridan.* Oxford: Clarendon Press, 2000.

Thomson, Peter. *Shakespeare's Professional Career.* Cambridge: Cambridge University Press, 1992.

Webster, Margaret. *Shakespeare without Tears.* New York: Whittlesey House, 1942.

Weimann, Robert. *Shakespeare and the Popular Tradition in the Theater: Studies in the Social Dimension of Dramatic Form and Function.* Edited by Robert Schwartz. Baltimore: Johns Hopkins University Press, 1978.

Wikander, Matthew H. *The Play of Truth and State: Historical Drama from Shakespeare to Brecht.* Baltimore: Johns Hopkins University Press, 1986.

Yachnin, Paul. *Stage-Wrights: Shakespeare, Jonson, Middleton, and the Making of Theatrical Value.* Philadelphia: University of Pennsylvania Press, 1997.

Biography

Halliday, F. E. *The Life of Shakespeare.* Rev. ed. London: Duckworth, 1964.

Honigmann, F. A. J. *Shakespeare: The "Lost Years."* 2d ed. Manchester: Manchester University Press, 1998.

Schoenbaum, Samuel. *Shakespeare's Lives.* New ed. Oxford: Clarendon Press, 1991.

————. *William Shakespeare: A Compact Documentary Life.* Oxford: Oxford University Press, 1977.

General

Bergeron, David M., and Geraldo U. de Sousa. *Shakespeare: A Study and Research Guide.* 3d ed. Lawrence: University of Kansas Press, 1995.

Berryman, John. *Berryman's Shakespeare.* Edited by John Haffenden. Preface by Robert Giroux. New York: Farrar, Straus and Giroux, 1999.

Bradbey, Anne, ed. *Shakespearian Criticism, 1919–35.* London: Oxford University Press, 1936.

Colie, Rosalie L. *Shakespeare's Living Art.* Princeton, N.J.: Princeton University Press, 1974.

Dean, Leonard F., ed. *Shakespeare: Modern Essays in Criticism.* Rev. ed. New York: Oxford University Press, 1967.

Grene, David. *The Actor in History: A Study in Shakespearean Stage Poetry.* University Park: Pennsylvania State University Press, 1988.

Goddard, Harold C. *The Meaning of Shakespeare.* 2 vols. Chicago: University of Chicago Press, 1951.

Kaufmann, Ralph J. *Elizabethan Drama: Modern Essays in Criticism.* New York: Oxford University Press, 1961.

McDonald, Russ. *The Bedford Companion to Shakespeare: An Introduction with Documents.* Boston: Bedford, 1996.

Raffel, Burton. *How to Read a Poem.* New York: Meridian, 1984.

Ricks, Christopher, ed. *English Drama to 1710.* Rev. ed. Harmondsworth: Sphere, 1987.

Siegel, Paul N., ed. *His Infinite Variety: Major Shakespearean Criticism Since Johnson.* Philadelphia: Lippincott, 1964.

Sweeting, Elizabeth J. *Early Tudor Criticism: Linguistic and Literary.* Oxford: Blackwell, 1940.

Van Doren, Mark. *Shakespeare.* New York: Holt, 1939.

Weiss, Theodore. *The Breath of Clowns and Kings: Shakespeare's Early Comedies and Histories.* New York: Atheneum, 1971.

Wells, Stanley, ed. *The Cambridge Companion to Shakespeare Studies.* Cambridge: Cambridge University Press, 1986.

FINDING LIST

Repeated unfamiliar words and meanings, alphabetically arranged, with act, scene, and footnote number of first occurrence, in the spelling (form) of that first occurrence

abide	3.1.49	*cause* (noun)	2.1.9
abuse (noun)	2.1.16	*chanced* (verb)	1.2.152
age (noun)	1.2.48	*chidden*	1.2.135
amiss	1.2.177	*closet* (noun)	2.1.32
annoying	1.3.16	*comfort* (verb)	2.1.166
answer (verb)	1.2.126	*conceited* (verb)	1.3.102
apt	2.2.31	*conjure*	1.2.102
audience	3.2.2	*constancy*	2.1.135
basest	1.1.54	*construe*	1.2.38
bayed	3.1.91	*content*	1.3.87
bear hard	1.2.201	*course*	1.2.7
bestow	1.3.96	*crossed*	1.2.138
betimes	2.1.75	*dear*	2.1.169
blood	3.2.59	*defend*	2.3.4
bondman	1.3.58	*determine*	4.1.2
boy	2.1.35	*discover*	1.2.51